Fix Your Cracks

Success Stems from Solid Foundations

By Jason Strong

Copyright

© 2020 Jason Strong

ISBN: 9798674571711

Study Aids

Actions speak louder than words, which is why this book provides free practical template documents to be used in conjunction with specific chapters. I have personally crafted and fine-tuned these aids after decades of chasing maximum productivity. I use these documents every day, and so should you if you are serious about eliciting real change into your lifestyle. They are effective tools for turning words into action, a vital component often missing from most books.

The first aid is a habit-building table that provides a guaranteed method to permanently reinforce good habits into your daily routine and should be referred to alongside chapter 1.3.

The second is a template for logically and efficiently setting goals, which should be referred to when reading chapter 1.4.

The third aid is a free ebook for a summary of the 10 most influential books that changed my perspectives and habits on my lifelong quest for self-improvement. If you were to heed the advice offered in all 10 of these books, your competency in all aspects of life would expand considerably, with success virtually guaranteed.

These study aids can be downloaded for free through the following link. They have significantly streamlined my life for many years. I am sure they will offer the same reward for you.

https://jason-strong.ck.page

Table of Contents

Introduction

Success isn't a mysterious phenomenon reserved only for the most talented and dedicated of people. Nor is it based entirely on luck and circumstance, although they certainly help. Rather, success results from the systematic application of fundamental concepts and principles that facilitate consistent progress, or what I term, the foundations of success. Failure occurs when we fail to apply these fundamentals, creating metaphoric cracks in our foundation.

This book is therefore dedicated to fixing the most common cracks that weaken our foundation and prevent us from reaching our full potential. Having dedicated a long career building some incredibly complex multi-billion-dollar construction projects, I know all too well the damage weak foundations cause, both physically and metaphorically.

My extensive experience in construction management has enabled me to develop a strong set of fundamental principles that allow for the construction of extremely complicated and multi-disciplinary projects. I have always drawn parallels with this to self-improvement. The skill of a project manager lies not only in technical competence but in breaking down extreme complexity into simple and actionable tasks. This book, therefore, brings the same approach; to break our large and often overwhelming goals and aspirations down into simple steps. The more simply we break down these mammoth tasks, the greater the chance of successfully completing them.

This book provides fundamental principles for five main topics: productivity, self-improvement, social skills, health, and finance. Although health and finance topics may seem out of place in a self-improvement book, poor physical and financial health will indirectly drag on your mental resilience. A deficiency in just one of these areas unbalances the whole equilibrium. Only when all five areas are as strong as they can possibly be, can you reach your full potential.

Much of the content in this book is not new. Habit creation and effective goal setting, for example, have been preached since self-help books first came to market. But where this book differs from others is in explaining the physiological reasons for why we do exactly what we do. It does not just scrape the surface of "what" but digs deeper into the "why". We all know to stop procrastinating, but unless we understand exactly why this inhibiting urge often overcomes us, we will never be able to truly tackle the source of the problem. Without aiming a fire extinguisher directly at the base of the fire, your time will be wasted fighting a never-ending battle. By aiming it straight at the base, however, the problem will be eliminated for good.

Visualize your competence as a concrete foundation underneath your house. If you want a multi-million-dollar property you need to ensure you build a strong enough foundation to accommodate it. The principles detailed in this book will provide you with the tools and knowledge needed to fix your cracks and strengthen your foundation. How high you wish to build is determined solely by how strong you build your foundation.

Throughout life, we all face the same unrelenting enemy; time. I was lucky to be introduced to these principles early in life where I was able to leverage them over time for compounding results. No matter your age, however, we can all still make the most of the time we have left. This book will provide one of the most concise guides available, drawing information from the hundreds of resources I have read and studied over the years, to boost your productivity and competence, providing you with the tools and knowledge needed to systematically achieve your goals.

There is far too much information to retain after just one reading, however. I recommend first reading the book in its entirety to understand how each of these principles relate to another. You will find key concepts linking separate principles together. Once finished, dedicate a week to each chapter to practice the techniques outlined within them. Remember, success is best achieved through simplicity, and small and consistent steps are the best way to remain dedicated. With each passing week, your competence will increase and your foundations will strengthen. And the sooner you start, the more time you will have to achieve greater things.

1. Productivity

1.1 Learn to Work with Your Emotions, Not Against Them.

Emotions can be both a blessing and a curse. One day you could be on top of the world having just graduated, procured your first job or witnessed the birth of a first child, whilst the very next day could send you into a state of shock; perhaps by the death of a loved one or an unfortunate redundancy. Emotions are so powerful they can be extremely difficult to control, leading to some regretful decisions that we might not have made had we thought more rationally about it. Whilst we cannot simply switch off our primal instincts, we can, and must, work towards being able to manage them. The rewards from mastering your emotions are extremely powerful and often defines the fine line between failure and success.

One shouldn't simply seek to ignore or block emotions altogether. They are an essential part of life, responsible for the fight or flight response and allowing us to build social relationships, both of which have allowed the human species to prosper. Yet left untamed, these same emotions can also be incredibly destructive, leading to overwhelm and depression. Our one basic primal urge is to survive at all costs, yet emotions can become so overwhelming that they lead death by suicide, the very thing these emotions are there to prevent. Emotions themselves, however, are not the fundamental issue. The real problem is our inability to understand them and, more importantly, how to rein them in when they start to stray off course and best utilize them to our benefit.

To understand our emotions, it is first important to understand how the brain works. English psychiatrist Dr Steve Peters explains in his groundbreaking book, The Chimp Paradox, that the human brain is divided into two distinct parts: the "human" and the "chimp". The human part of the brain is located in the frontal lobe and thinks and acts based on logic and facts. The other part of the brain, the chimp, lives in the limbic system and its functions are primitive and reactionary. Whereas the chimp, who is responsible for the flight or fight reaction, acts extremely rapidly in response to perceived threats, the human side of the brain is much slower to react. The highly cognitive area analyses carefully and is more detail orientated.

Both parts of the brain are essential to human life. The chimp is highly reactive and easily stimulated. This part of the brain developed over thousands of years of biological evolution to increase survival rates in the species. Before humans lived in the relative safety of modern civilizations, they relied on this limbic system to react quickly enough to dangerous stimuli. If faced with a predator, for example, there is little time to analyze the situation rationally; instead, the body has developed a highly reactive emotional output which is capable of responding much more rapidly. When identifying a potentially dangerous situation, the highly reactive chimp fires a sharp burst of adrenaline, triggering the fight or flight response that allows humans to best deal with imminent threats. We developed an emotional mechanism because it could induce quicker responses to potential dangers than the more logical, but slower, human counterpart.

Whilst the inner chimp is vitally important for human survival, many of the emotional responses elicited by our chimps are overblown in today's society because humans have invented far faster than they have evolved. Where emotions like fear once used to be vital for surviving in the wild, they are needed far less often in modern society. Unfortunately, our chimp hasn't adapted to these more modern environments and still evaluates the world as if we were still primal. Of course, we still have plenty to fear, but our threats are not usually immediate, like a predator, but more distant, such as financial troubles or poor health. In these more modern scenarios, logical reactions would be more valuable in solving these problems than split-second emotional ones. Yet unfortunately, the chimp reacts before we can even start to rationally analyze the situation. For example, the thought of flying fills many with extreme fear and anxiety, even though the chances of dying while flying are just one in 11 million. Yet these same people think nothing of driving a car, in which you are over 2,200 times more likely to die (1 in 5000 according to a Harvard University study). The rational part of the brain may know this, yet it still doesn't overcome the strong emotional reaction to not get on that plane. Even the human brain, the most intelligent in the animal kingdom, cannot overpower the brute force of emotion.

One of the main focuses of Dr Steve Peters' book is the constant battle between these opposing sides of the brain. Although the chimp is not as relevant today as it once was, the sheer speed and magnitude of emotional reactions often overwhelm the rational brain. Road rage is a prime example of these two systems at war. A driver cuts you off and gives you the finger. The rational side of you knows that there is absolutely nothing to be gained by engaging in road rage; this person means nothing to you and will most likely never be seen again. Reacting aggressively not only increases your chances of getting involved in an accident but also puts other nearby drivers at risk. Yet the chimp sees this driver as opposition; a primitive alpha male rivalry. The speed and strength of the chimp often lead to emotions dominating our decisions before the rational brain has a chance to analyze them. The same is true with arguments. A small comment or nasty email can send your inner-chimp into haywire, resulting in an immediate argument or counter email we usually regret once the human brain finally gets its chance to assess the situation.

"Your inner Chimp is too powerful for you to control, but you can manage it", explains British psychiatrist Steve Peters. Becoming the best version of yourself requires an ability to rein in these limbic reactive emotions as quickly as possible before you act on them in a way you later regret. The first step towards achieving this is to simply acknowledge your emotions for what they are. Understand that whenever a stressful event occurs, what you feel at that moment, whether it be fear or anger, is perfectly normal. It is your limbic system trying to protect you the only way it knows how; extremely quickly and forcefully. We have no control over how the limbic system chooses to react, it is beyond our immediate control. What we can control, however, with time and practice, is the way we physically act upon these emotions. Understand that the initial rush of emotions is a result of the limbic system, or the chimp part of the brain. Your inner-chimp does not define who you are, that is the job of the human part of the brain. In other words, we can only control the way we act, not how we react. By simply reaffirming this to yourself every time an emotional situation appears, it can help calm the chimp and engage the human side faster.

For minor incidents, the simple act of recognizing when the chimp is driving decisions may be enough to stop it dead in its tracks. For more emotion-inducing events, however, Dr Peters suggests two methods for gaining control over the chimp as quickly as possible. The first method is to distract it. When overcome with emotion from the driver who cut you off, for example, find a way to distract your chimp. Whether it be by talking to your passenger or singing along to the radio, find another emotional task for your chimp to focus on. When stressed by a tough day at work, hit the gym for a hard workout. The chimp will always prioritize the most imminent "threat", helping to divert attention away from other stressful scenarios. This is why exercise is such an effective way to destress; your chimp won't have the capacity to be mad at that snide email when your heart is pounding at 180 bpm.

For more severe situations, however, there is no amount of distraction that will diffuse the chimp. Perhaps you have lost your job or messed up an interview for that college you always wanted to get into. Here, Dr Peters suggests "boxing" the chimp by metaphorically capturing it in a box. You cannot place a hyperactive and angry chimp straight in a box, however, for it will force his way out with all its might. First, you have to exhaust the chimp by simply letting it vent. Let these thoughts of anger and emotion flow through your mind. Don't hold back, just let it vent as hard and as quickly as it can. Like letting rip on a punchbag, eventually, you will tire and the initial emotion will have subsided. Once these thoughts have been released and vented, and the chimp has tired, you can then "box" it to allow the "human" system to take back control.

Only by practicing mindfulness of when your limbic chimp is driving your decisions and taking over your actions will you gradually begin to manage your emotions. To recap, the first step when overwhelmed by emotion is to recognize who is controlling your thoughts, the chimp or the human? If you are behaving in a way you would rather not, it is most likely the chimp taking over. For less significant moments, the simple act of recognizing that the chimp is directing your thoughts is enough to engage your human brain and regain control of your actions. Remember, you cannot hold yourself responsible for the thoughts from the chimp, they occur far too fast for us to be able to control. But we are responsible for our actions, which we must try to direct from the human part of the brain and not the chimp. If this fails, find ways to distract your chimp. For more stressful situations, distraction is not enough and the chimp needs to be "boxed". To tire the chimp, allow it to vent by encouraging your thoughts and emotions to run free. Don't be embarrassed or ashamed of these thoughts, they are beyond your control, remember. Soon, the chimp will tire and you can "box" it and manually engage your rational human part of the brain. Remember that you are not your feelings; you are your actions. Some people naturally have more control over their feelings where others have to work harder at it. In the end, it doesn't matter, only the results do. You do not have to act on your feelings, they are just suggestions. Being able to control them first depends on you understanding this and recognizing it as quickly as possible when the chimp inevitably starts taking over.

The human-chimp brain divide is an incredibly revealing concept that has resulted in one of the largest transformations of my life. Such is the power of the chimp, however, that the battle is lifelong. We can become progressively better at managing it, but no one is ever able to master it. Emotions are so rapid and compelling that there will always be those moments where it overwhelms us before we can analyze the situation rationally. These two parts of the brain have a broader influence on many of our tendencies, such as whether we build good or bad habits or whether we focus on our goals or tend to procrastinate. We will see this human-chimp concept throughout the rest of this book where most of our habits, good or bad, link back to this basic science of emotion vs. logic. I highly recommend picking up a copy of "The Chimp Paradox" by Dr Steve Peters, one of the most influential books of its time.

Task:

Make a list of recent events or situations where you reacted in a way you now wish you hadn't. Was it road rage, aggressively responding to a snide email, or arguing with your spouse? If you now regret how you conducted yourself, even if you know you were in the right, then your chimp was most likely responding before your human had a chance to process the situation.

Keep making daily notes on when and why such reactive events occurred and how you could have avoided the chimp from driving your actions. An excellent tip is to just walk away for five minutes, take a few deep breaths and let the chimp vent. Let all those thoughts and emotions, no matter how nasty, float around your head. Remember, thoughts and actions can be completely separate. You are not held responsible for your thoughts as they are beyond your control. Only your actions define you. Let your chimp fight that mental punch bag as hard as it can until it tires itself out.

Once tired, distract or box it and let your human take control. The human is better able to think about the situation holistically, such as the advantages and disadvantages of any decision you might make. Best of all you avoid making a decision that will land you in greater trouble, further aggravating the chimp. Taking these steps will eventually allow you to take greater and greater control of your chimp whilst increasing your mental resilience, a trait that helps in all walks of life.

1.2 Overcoming Overwhelm

The San peoples, indigenous hunter-gatherers of Southern Africa, are the personification of relentlessness. Using what is considered the oldest of all hunting techniques, persistence hunting, these incredible specimens catch their prey by outenduring them. After grueling chases lasting over eight hours, they finally claim their prize when their prey hasn't the strength to physically move any longer.

Ever since learning of these inspiring peoples, they always come to mind whenever I feel myself falling victim to procrastination, for it too is an enemy that never relents. Left untamed, procrastination can swallow endless chunks of time, wasting this precious finite resource forever. Like a deer falling prey to the Sans peoples, the feeling of looming procrastination chases you, often to the point where it outendures you. But once we understand exactly why the urge to procrastinate is so strong, we can find techniques to stay ahead of it no matter how long it chases.

Many believe procrastination to be a modern problem. With the advent of social welfare and the internet, the consequences of sitting on the couch avoiding the realities of accountability seem less severe than they perhaps once were. Yet procrastination has plagued man since they could first think for themselves. The Greek poet Hesiod, writing around 800 B.C., cautioned not to "put your work off till tomorrow and the day after." The Roman consul Cicero called procrastination "hateful in the conduct of affairs".

Procrastination is the greatest threat to productivity. We can have the best intentions in the world - many try to avoid procrastinating by setting a to-do list accounting for every waking hour - but this alone is not enough to overcome the temptation to delay what we know needs to be done. We know we need to sit down and finish those tax returns before it's too late, yet something keeps us glued to the television against our better knowledge. What's worse, the feeling of guilt, having put off what we know needs to be done now, far outweighs the small pleasure rewarded for the immediate gratification resulting from procrastinating.

As with many human flaws, the root cause of procrastination can be traced back to the emotional chimp. The chimp is only satisfied when it is comfortable, and therefore seeks immediate gratification and pleasure. This need for immediate gratification often triggers an intense battle between the limbic system (the unconscious zone that includes the pleasure center) and the prefrontal cortex (a much more recently evolved part of the brain that's basically your internal "planner"). You know you need to sit down and write that report, but your chimp knows it won't be fun or comfortable and would rather you participate in something more immediately gratifying, such as scrolling through social media for three hours. When the limbic system wins, which is often, the result is putting off for what could (and should) be done now, offering a temporary relief from that uncomfortable feeling of working on something which isn't as gratifying.

The real danger here is not the immediate failure of the task you were supposed to complete, however. Rather it is the creation of a (negative) habit loop each time you allow the chimp to win. The chimp's reward of immediate gratification arising from the act of procrastination creates a loop that reacts in the same way, every time you come across this same trigger. For example, every time you put off that evening run, your chimp becomes accustomed to the burst of immediate gratification when you find something more immediately gratifying, yet unproductive, to the chimp, such as scrolling through social media. When you next think about going for a run, your chimp automatically associates the thought of you running with the immediate gratification that it can expect to follow: scrolling through social media. Every iteration of this trigger-reward loop makes the negative habit even stronger and harder to break.

So, what causes this urge to procrastinate? Why do we avoid what we know needs doing right now to seek this sense of immediate gratification, even when we know we will feel worse for not doing it?

As you may have guessed from the title of this chapter; the answer is overwhelm (disclaimer: although overwhelm is not technically a noun I will be using it as one from here on in the interest of clarity). Overwhelm is the fundamental reason why many fail to overcome procrastination no matter how many self-help books they read or however hard they try to fight it. It is incredibly difficult to regain focus and productivity once overwhelm has taken over. Instead, the best chance of avoiding it is to get ahead of it.

Overwhelm is what clouds judgment, induces fear, and sends your emotions into haywire. My favorite definition of overwhelm is to be buried or drowned beneath a huge mass. This "huge mass" is a metaphor for the unknown; we all know that feeling of having too much to do in too little time, or when life just seems to keep dealing you bad hands with no respite. The end is out of sight and it feels like you're trapped in an endless cycle of frustration. The result is almost always stress, which wears down your mental resilience and ability to remain focused. I visualize overwhelm as a mental fog. Imagine you have to run a marathon in thick fog where it is impossible to see further than the end of your hand. With no visual clues as to how long you have been running, or how long you have left to run, and your exhausted body and mind are screaming for you to stop, remaining in control of your thoughts and emotions to finish the race becomes orders of magnitude more difficult than if you could see the light at the end of the tunnel. Without the mile markers, finish line, or supporting crowd cheering you on, the marathon becomes a more mentally demanding battle between the chimp and you. Questions like "I am exhausted, how long have I got left?" cannot be answered when your mind is lost in this fog, frustrating your chimp, and encouraging it to persuade you to give up.

This "mind fog" is how I visualize the effects of overwhelm. Whether it be a marathon, an essay, or starting a business, not knowing where you currently are or where the finish line lies makes every situation seem much more daunting. Confusion often leads to frustration, which makes the chimp uncomfortable, sending it into a fit of fury. It is extremely difficult to diffuse the chimp once frustrated and regain control of your emotions. The mind fog sends toxic negative thoughts, such as "why am I doing this?", "I'm not strong enough" and "this is too much for me" bouncing around your mind like a pinball machine with each bounce multiplying the frustration. We have all been through this barrage of emotions at some point or another and it isn't productive.

Overwhelm not only prevents us from following through with our goals and ambitions, it often prevents us from attempting them at all. Say you wanted to create your own business. Hundreds of questions would instantly appear, each with the potential to cause crippling confusion and overwhelm. Where do I start? How do I get a business license? How much capital do I need to raise? How many sales are needed to keep cash flow positive? Where does one find employees willing to work at a startup? How many months can one last without sales before cash flow dries up? What happens if I fail? Will the bank take my house? Where will my family live? With so many unknowns leading to further unknowns, confusion and frustration are inevitable. When you cannot visualize the direct path to reach your end goal, your mind fogs up, starts racing and the chimp, feeding on your frustration, dominates your emotions in a bid to prevent you from thinking these unpleasant thoughts. It is here where you are overwhelmed and are likely to start procrastinating and avoid taking the necessary actions needed to achieve your goals.

Overwhelm stems from two main sources. Firstly, it is from the fear of the unknown. Many do not know how they are going to pay their next rent bill or fear a presentation to a room full of people who they are not familiar with. The inherent negativity bias in humans (the notion that things of a more negative nature have a greater impact on us than those which are positive) sends the mind pacing through all the worst-case scenarios that could occur, even if the chances of them happening are slim. We soon become overwhelmed by "analysis paralysis" where we overthink all the potential situations that could occur, no matter how unlikely. The fog has descended, we cannot see the finish line and tasks seem that much more daunting because of it. Even simple tasks such as fixing a leaky faucet can seem daunting enough to those inexperienced in plumbing to avoid even trying altogether. In response to these fears of the unknown, and not being able to see the finish line (mind fog), the chimp will always be on hand to offer you a comfortable, albeit counterproductive, way out.

The second source of overwhelm is the fear of exactly what is known. Physical challenges are a prime example, such as that 5-mile run in the morning you know is going to feel torturous. Or that month-end report you know takes four mind-numbing hours to complete. Again, at the first sign of discomfort and overwhelm, the chimp charges into action, trying its hardest to offer you a comfortable way out right now, as opposed to the feeling of comfort later having completed your task despite the short-term pain involved.

Both these sources of overwhelm, however, result in the same fundamental emotion that stimulates the chimp into action; fear. Fear, whether it be that of the known or the unknown, is what drives discomfort, frustration, and hence procrastination. The limbic system is inherently designed to avoid these feelings of discomfort instantaneously, no matter how beneficial the task may be at a later date.

Despite the crippling effects overwhelm can rein down upon us, over 627,000 people each year overcome it and go on to start a business of their own. What enables some plucky entrepreneurs to persevere through so many unknowns where many wouldn't even start? It is through a combination of thorough planning and the simple act of mindfulness. Every single entrepreneur will at some point have had feelings of overwhelm and hopelessness. Yet the simple act of being mindful of these emotions enables you to recognize that these feelings are natural. The chimp is hardwired into your genetic fabric and cannot be wished away. Do not concern yourself with this chimp, he will be there no matter what. We are judged not on the emotional thoughts of the chimp, but on the rational actions of the human side of the brain. Do not beat yourself up about negative thoughts derived from the chimp. We do not choose them and cannot stop them. We can, however, control our rational thoughts and hence our actions.

Mindfulness is defined as the act of rationalizing your emotional thoughts and viewing them in the appropriate context. Part of this rationalizing process includes understanding that these emotional thoughts are normal and inevitable. Every single person, no matter how successful, will be bombarded by these thoughts just as often as anyone else. By being mindful, however, they are able to better focus on their awareness in the present moment and understand the context surrounding these thoughts. For those who are terrible with constant snacking, understand that it is the chimp who is seeking immediate gratification and this is normal; these thoughts occur far too quickly for us to control. It is not a judgment of your character or mental resolve; they would be occurring even in the strongest of wills. Those who appear better able to resist snacking may seem mentally superior, but in actuality, they are simply more mindful that their emotions are separate from their actions. Mindfulness helps convert these emotional feelings of instant gratification into suggestions as opposed to commands. It also snaps the chimp out of autopilot and allows the rational mind a chance to make a decision before it's too late.

To aid mindfulness, ask yourself this one simple question every time procrastination or overwhelm looms; "what is at stake here?". For that cookie, what is at stake is gaining weight and failing your meal plan. For smoking, it is the very real fact that every cigarette increases your chances of lung cancer. Avoiding that monthly report increases feelings of guilt and results in a lower quality, rushed end product. Mindfulness can help us contextualize the true cost of procrastination, and if these feelings of discomfort are greater than the immediate need for gratification, we can shock the chimp into changing its focus. The chimp will always focus on the biggest discomfort.

Mindfulness is a reactive technique for dealing with overwhelm. A proactive approach is also necessary in order to minimize the sense of overwhelm occurring in the first place. We do this through thorough planning and task setting in order to minimize the number of unknowns which cause the initial overwhelm. By setting goals and tasks in sufficient detail (such as the what, when, and hows), the path from point A to point B can be more easily visualized. If your goal is to lose weight, for example, the strategy of simply eating less is not detailed enough. Instead, each and every meal must be planned in advance so you can see exactly what is required to reach your goal. There is far less thinking involved when everything is already laid out in front of you and there is, therefore, less opportunity for the chimp to interfere. Writing this book is no different. Admittedly my first book took me three years to write as I did not set tasks in sufficient detail to keep me on track. When a difficult chapter arose, the overwhelm from not knowing exactly how I would tackle the tough chapter induced procrastination. This book, however, has taken me much less time, as I structured my tasks into small enough chunks to ensure the endpoint was always in view. For example, I know my book would be around 60,000 words. So, I would set myself a task of writing 600 words a day. Every day I could tangibly measure how far away I was from the finish line which boosted my motivation and kept the chimp firmly out of sight.

The skill here is breaking down goals into small enough pieces to provide enough detail to clear the fog. In construction we break down large projects, say building a 20-mile road, into small enough activities where we can price each individual aspect of labor, materials, and equipment. If you break down your goals and still can't visualize exactly how you will complete each of these smaller tasks, then it hasn't been broken down enough and overwhelm will likely arise. It is worth noting that different people are able to break down goals to different degrees. Steve Jobs, a founder of Apple, was infamous for being spontaneous. I'm sure he didn't have a large breakdown identifying each and every step required to reach his goals. But his vision was so strong, and his resources so great, that he didn't need to break it down into such small steps. His finish line was so vivid in his mind the point of overwhelm would occur with less intensity than that for most others. Jobs also had a strong army of workers able to deliver his vision, so his end goal (creating the ultimate tech company) needed only big steps (e.g. create iPhone) which he handed down to his employees. His employees, however, would have needed a massive breakdown down to a nanoscopic transistor level in order to build the iPhone.

The following two chapters are dedicated entirely to building a system that enables you to break down goals into small enough tasks where overwhelm can be eliminated as much as possible. These techniques rely on two powerful concepts; setting goals effectively and consistently achieving them through the forging of strong habits. Effective use of these two techniques provides one of the most powerful systems I have found in combating overwhelm and procrastination and therefore boosting productivity significantly.

Task:

Recall those moments where you have previously succumbed to procrastination. Recollect how the guilt experienced having put off your task was often far more intense and longer lasting than the immediate gratification.

Knowing that procrastination is a result of overwhelm from the fear of what lies ahead, identify possible sources of knowns and unknowns that may have caused you to give up on your goals. For those struggling to stick to diets, it could be the unknown of how long you need to stick to your diet and the lack of finish line. For those who are struggling to prepare for a long-distance race, it could be the upcoming known pain involved in all those hours of grueling practice.

In response, remember the two steps to combating them. The first to proactively set goals and tasks in sufficient detail to clear your mind of this fog and enable you to visualize your exact path from point A to point B (as outlined in the next two chapters). By clarifying how you will get from Point A to Point B we reduce overwhelm from the source.

Even with the best planning in the world, life's curveballs will always test your ability to persevere at some point or another. Here we draw upon the second technique; the more reactive task of mindfulness. Remind yourself that you are not to be held accountable for these thoughts; the chimp is a separate entity who is simply dwelling in your mind. You are not defined by your thoughts, only your actions.

1.3 Habits - The Foundation of Productivity

Habits are to productivity what tires are to a bicycle; without them, you won't be getting anywhere fast no matter how hard you pedal. Good habits keep us on track and minimize the chances of succumbing to procrastination. Many misunderstand what is involved in creating and maintaining habits; they believe habits require sheer willpower to maintain, such as forcing yourself to exercise every day. This couldn't be any further from the truth. The beauty of habits is that they shift mental resources away from the part of the brain that draws upon willpower and onto the part which acts autonomously. Many repetitive tasks, such as eating, washing, and even driving, when performed consistently, eventually become highly automated. The brain is incredibly adaptive and consistently looks for ways to make tasks more efficient. Anyone who has driven to work only to arrive and realize they cannot remember the drive itself knows this feeling. When you perform activities consistently enough, your brain learns to perform them on autopilot. The beauty here is that the less thinking that's involved, the less chance the chimp has to interfere.

"The difference between an amateur and a professional is in their habits. An amateur has amateur habits. A professional has professional habits."— Steven Pressfield, American Author. The appearance of superhuman levels of self-discipline is simply a collection of strong habits, carefully cultivated over time. Overnight success is a myth perpetuated by biographies that spare you the boring details of the incredible amount of time successful people spend making and breaking habits. Much like how a building can only be built as tall as its foundations allow, humans can only become as productive as their foundational habits allow.

Humans are, by nature, creatures of habit. Around 45 percent of our reported tasks on a given day are performed habitually without much thought, including breathing, eating, making a coffee, and washing our hands after using the bathroom. They all occur subconsciously without us having to think too hard about them as they have been ingrained into us for so long. Furthermore, because these habits occur automatically outside the spectrum of thought, it is difficult to realize how prevalent and influential they really are. But without them, our brains would be forever occupied on performing menial tasks.

Whenever you initiate a thought the brain transmits this thought through electrical impulses called neurons to the corresponding part of the body. For example, when picking up a cup of coffee, the brain processes the thought of lifting your arm and passes it via a network of neurons to the muscles in your arm. The brain, however, being one of the most capable and efficient processors in existence, works out the easiest and most efficient way to perform this task. Every repetition allows the brain to fine-tune the movement to enable further repetitions to become even more efficient. This is the fundamental mechanism of the biological learning process, such as how riding a bike becomes easier the more it is repeated. The same system is at play with habits. The brain recognizes repeated behavior and, in a bid to make the process as efficient as possible, starts to link the thought to the action automatically. The purpose of this is to reduce the number of cognitive resources spent on menial tasks and free them up for tasks of higher cognitive importance. Habits effectively allow our brains to outsource some of the grunt work of decision making to other less critical parts of the brain in order to enable us to become much more efficient thinkers.

Neuroscientists have traced these automated habit-making behaviors to a part of the brain called the basal ganglia, which also plays a key role in the development of emotions, memories, and pattern recognition. Decisions, meanwhile, are made in a different part of the brain called the prefrontal cortex. As a behavior becomes increasingly automated through repetition, the decision-making prefrontal cortex transfers the process to the automated basal ganglia. The basal ganglia, one of the oldest structures in our brain, is completely exempt from the process of thinking and acts as a biological autopilot to free up cognitive capacity for more pressing tasks. Ideally, we want to seek to transfer new habits away from the cognitive prefrontal cortex and onto the automated basal ganglia.

Understanding the underlying science behind habits allows us to create a framework for how to best create them. The habit loop; a helpful framework originating from "The Power of Habit" by Charles Duhigg, deconstructs a habit into three fundamental components:

1. **Triggers** - the environmental details which your brain has previously associated with a habit. Triggers set the habit loop in motion by sending our brain into autopilot.

2. **Behaviors** - the actual habit response exhibited. Behaviors can be either actions performed externally or reactive patterns of thought. Behaviors can also be good or bad.

3. **Rewards** - Rewards reinforce a habit, causing our brain to strengthen the associated link between the trigger and the behavior. Rewards can be anything, such as a small candy for completing a workout, or a coffee having just completed your weekly report. Perhaps it can even be the satisfaction of knowing you have completed your behavior and don't need to worry about it anymore. It just needs to be something that releases feelings of enjoyment and reward to close the habit loop.

Triggers, behaviors, and rewards are the three points of leverage utilized when creating, strengthening, or eliminating habits. Habits can, therefore, be created, altered, or broken by focusing on our current habit bottleneck, the "weakest link" of the three.

A trigger is defined as an event that kicks off the automatic urge to complete a habit. Triggers are the key to forming new habits and breaking old ones. Simply put, triggers encourage the habit behavior to happen. Smokers who wish to quit often fail because of this strong trigger, such as the smell of a cigarette, or simply being bored. Every time a smoker encounters this trigger, they will be hit with the urge to smoke. Each time this trigger is answered with the behavior (the act of smoking), neural pathways reinforce this trigger-behavior link, and the (bad) habit of smoking every time a cigarette is smelled becomes stronger with each repetition. This associative process is described in neuroscience as Hebbian learning, and is summarized by "neurons that fire together, wire together." As an association between a habit and a trigger increases, the habit becomes increasingly ingrained until it can be performed automatically by the basal ganglia. This is true of both good and bad habits.

If you wish to break bad habits, therefore, you need to list the potential triggers that may be initiating it. Whenever this bad habit is performed, make a note of what you were doing, where you were or the exact time the habit occurred. If you find yourself unable to resist the temptation of a cigarette, make a note of what you were doing the moment you first had the craving. Did you just receive a stressful email? Perhaps stress is your trigger. Just turned 3 p.m? Maybe time is your trigger. Did some of your colleagues just go for a smoke break? Perhaps social bonding triggers your cravings. Whatever it is, you need to identify your triggers before you can successfully break a habit.

As the trigger-habit association strengthens, the habit becomes increasingly automated. Over time and with repetition, the habit becomes easier to stick to, whether it is productive or not. Studies have shown that people perform automated behaviors — like pulling out of a driveway or brushing teeth — the same way every single time if they're in the same environment causing the same trigger. But if they change the environment, such as taking a vacation, it's likely that the behavior will change as the trigger is no longer present in this new environment.

It's also a great reason why vacations have proved to be one of the most effective ways to break bad habits. If you wish to quit smoking, you should stop smoking while you're on a vacation — because all your old triggers and rewards aren't there anymore. You now have the opportunity to form a new habit loop and are more able to carry it over into your everyday life, so long as you make the effort to remove the previous trigger once back home.

So, it is clear that triggers need to be eliminated to break bad habits, often by changing the environment in which these triggers usually occur. In creating new triggers, however, there are four general tips to follow to ensure they are successful. They need to be specific, unavoidable, consistent, and automatic. You can remember these as SUCA, which is what you will be if you try to create a trigger that doesn't follow these four components.

A specific trigger means leaving no room for interpretation. For example, "take a walk in the evening" is too vague. Instead, "take a walk at 8 p.m." is specific. "In the evening" could be anytime between 5-8 p.m. and the lack of a specific time leaves more opportunity for delay, making it harder to build a reliable trigger.

An unavoidable trigger means it is impossible to avoid encountering it. For example, if the habit you wish to build is to go to the gym every day, you cannot place the trigger at say lunchtime where you cannot guarantee you will have time to go. Instead, time it before or after work when you know you will always have time.

A consistent trigger occurs at a reliable frequency. We have already seen how habits are strengthened primarily through repetition. Without the trigger occurring frequently, the brain cannot build a strong trigger-behavior link.

Finally, the trigger should be automatic, where it can occur on its own with little to no ongoing effort. Some may set a trigger for taking medicine at 9:30 a.m. but time by itself is not a reliable trigger as it can be easily missed if you are distracted or busy. Setting an alarm for 9:30 a.m., however, is automatic as you don't have to make an effort to remember. Once you hear your alarm the habit will be triggered automatically.

A common habit many wish to build is reading consistently every day. My foolproof habit process for reading is as follows. Firstly, a strong trigger needs to be created. Remember it needs to be specific, unavoidable, consistent, and automatic (SUCA). A strong trigger would therefore be to read 20 pages at 6:30 AM every day. This is specific with no room for interpretation. I wake up at 6 a.m. so it is unavoidable. This behavior occurs every day, so it is consistent. Finally, I place the book on the kitchen table where I eat breakfast, so it is automatic; I start reading once I finish my meal. Together, this creates a strong trigger where the habit of reading every day can be effectively implemented.

To ensure these triggers are repeated consistently, I have created a habit table document which is a simple table with boxes to check every time a repetition of the behavior is completed (e.g. reading) up to 50 repetitions. The aim of this document is to ensure consistency with your trigger, which is the most common source of failure when building habits. I have made the exact document I use available for download at https://jason-strong.ck.page. This simple but effective table will become the backbone of your habit-building process and should be placed wherever it is most unavoidable, such as on the fridge, next to your bed or on the bathroom mirror. Only after you have ticked off the 50th iteration without missing a repetition will the habit have become automated. If you fail, as can easily occur if this concept is new to you, start again from day one. If you are serious about creating the habit, you have to be honest with yourself.

Finally, plan a reward every time a repetition of your habit is completed. Whenever I finish my 600 words of writing, for example, I reward myself with a 30-minute coffee break. For smaller tasks, the simple act of crossing it off the list rewards me with a sense of progress. Chocolate, television, or scrolling through social media can all be used as a reward. It can be whatever you want as long as it is genuinely rewarding and manipulates the chimp into associating the trigger with a reward, therefore encouraging it to perform the trigger without you having to fight it.

Habit-forming is an incredibly deep scientific process that goes far beyond this chapter. There is only so far one can delve into this process without dedicating a whole book to it. I recommend reading other books on the topic, such as "Atomic Habits" by James Clear and "The Power of Habit" by Charles Duhigg. These books delve much deeper into the habit-building process and offer step by step advice to make, or break, them. Remember, habit building is not a one-time effort but a learnable meta-skill that must be practiced for life. If your daily habits require discipline to execute, you're doing them wrong. With a habit-centric approach, we don't "do things" as much as "make the things we want to do easier to do in the future, each time we do it".

Task:

Think of a habit you would love to create. Perhaps reading, exercising, or eating five portions of fruits and vegetables a day. Create your trigger for this habit. Remember it must be specific, unavoidable, consistent, and automatic (SUCA). Set an alarm to trigger it if you have to. Next create a reward, whatever it may be to encourage the completion of the trigger-behavior-reward loop. All three components of this must be present. You may be able to force yourself to do the behavior without a reward, but you will not reinforce it as a habit and therefore never transfer the task to the automated part of the brain, which is the real aim here.

Print off my habit table, or create your own, and write your habit and trigger in the left-hand column. Create 50 checkboxes next to it which must be completed at the frequency in which you defined it in the consistency component of your trigger. Make sure you tick it off every day (or whatever your consistent durations are) without fail. If you miss one, analyze which part of SUCA was missing, amend and start again.

Once you have completed 50 consecutive repetitions, the habit should now be highly automated. You shouldn't have to force yourself to perform it and the trigger will now be deep in your subconscious. Often, you will find your subconscious, a creature of habit, screaming out for you to complete the task even if you try to avoid it.

1.4 How to Effectively Set Goals

Of all the habits one should build, effective goal setting should be at the very top of the list. There are hundreds of books all touting the importance of setting goals, yet many still fail to cement this illusive habit permanently into their lifestyle. Combined with the knowledge of how to properly create and maintain habits (by utilizing all three parts of the trigger loop using SUCA triggers as mentioned in the previous chapter), the goal-setting techniques explained below, henceforth known as "The System", will enable your productivity to skyrocket.

There are hundreds of metaphors expressing just how important goals are in life. I have always compared them to sailing across a large ocean without a compass. It is inevitable that such a journey will face a great number of storms and take a long time to eventually cross, most likely ending alone on the bottom of the seabed. Almost every self-help book on the market has a passage of text expressing the importance of goals, so the concept is hopefully not new to you. But most books fail to provide a systematic and foolproof method for effectively setting and following through with your goals.

Effectively planned goals are what separates the likes of the super successful, such as Richard Branson, Elon Musk, and Walt Disney, from the rest of us mere mortals. The vision of their goals, and the resulting emotion arisen from them, is what allows for such intense focus and relentlessness in chasing them. Anyone can write goals on a piece of paper, but being emotionally charged by them is a completely different sensation.

I believe there are two key reasons why most goals are never realized. Firstly, they are simply the wrong goals or expressed in the wrong way. Many want to become a millionaire by age 30 but this goal misses the most essential component of any goal; emotion. Money alone is not a strong enough driver of emotion to hold our focus through the relentless failures and rejection ambitious goals contain. Those who make great fortunes usually stumble upon it as a by-product of their actual goal, such as creating the world's best product or service, a goal which conjures much more emotion than the simple act of becoming wealthy. Steve Job's financial success came as a byproduct of his ultimate goal of building an enduring company that prioritized people. Everything else — products and profits — while still important, were secondary. All goals must contain a strong emotional driver.

The second reason why goals are often abandoned is due to improper planning of precisely how these goals will be implemented to completion. Without a strategic plan defining exactly how you will turn your dreams into action, the results will always be inconsistent. Effective goal setting is not magic; it does not turn you into an unrelenting force that is suddenly capable of focusing on nothing but your goal. Rather it is a systematic process that allows for consistent action and results through strategic and efficient use of time. It is more of a science that must be learned and practiced.

An estimated 95 percent of diets fail. I am willing to bet that most of those who failed did so because they tried to tackle too much too quickly without breaking down their goal into sufficiently manageable bite-sized chunks. Positive change, whether it be losing weight or starting a business, requires time and patience. Very rarely is there some sort of "get rich quick" scheme that will achieve your goals without requiring long-term dedication. Unfortunately, humans are inherent short-term thinkers, and the chimp requires immediate gratification. Waking up at 5 a.m. every morning to run for an hour only to lose a few pounds every week or so is not fun, and most fail early on when the realization that change often takes time dawns upon them. Unsustainable long-term use of willpower is forced, as opposed to investing time in creating sustainable long-term habits. "Fail to prepare, prepare to fail" is just as true when it comes to setting goals.

The limbic system (the chimp) is once again the main culprit for why dedication to long-term goals seems so elusive to many. Humans are hardwired for short-term thinking from their hunter-gatherer days when we only concerned ourselves with our immediate environment. We therefore have to present our goals to the chimp in this same short-term fashion. By breaking down long-term goals into shorter bite-size pieces, we remove much of the discomfort experienced by the chimp who demands more instant gratification. It is much easier for the chimp to read 10 pages a day of a 100-page book for 10 consecutive days than it is for it to read 100 pages all in one go. Your chimp receives his instant gratification having read the 10-page goal and is much more willing to do the same tomorrow. The time taken to read the book is the same either way, perhaps 30 minutes for every 10 pages read (five hours total), but by splitting the goal into smaller achievable goals, the whole process is a lot less daunting to the limbic system and the ultimate goal much more likely to be completed. We need to be strategic in our goal setting to align them with the needs of the limbic system. By reading fewer pages in one sitting, but reading more consistently, and therefore frequently rewarding the chimp through the habit loop, you are much more likely to build the habit of reading and ultimately read more as a result. There is a tradeoff in that these habits take time to first build, usually in the span of months. But if you are serious in committing to creating new habits, which often last a lifetime, then time must first be dedicated in order to wire your brain into a new way of thinking.

Many believe goal setting is a fanciful notion but the benefits are unavoidable. Firstly, goals provide a real sense of purpose, motivation, and direction. Remember the foggy finish line analogy? You are much more likely to complete a marathon when you know exactly why this goal is so important and you can clearly see the mile markers to track your progress. Running through a thick fog, where you are unable to see where you are or how far you have left to push, makes quitting much more likely. When your uncomfortable and frustrated chimp inevitably asks "why are you here?" and "why don't you give up?", your well-defined and emotionally charged goals will immediately provide you with an instant response: "I'm not giving up because I have been training for a year and want to prove to myself that I am mentally tough". Having these answers on hand, by visualizing your goals and understanding exactly why they are important to you, is a powerful tool in wrestling with your chimp.

Secondly, well-defined goals provide focus and avoid the urge to procrastinate. We have already seen how overwhelm, or the lack of planning and a clear focus on your goals, leads to procrastination without fail. You can have all the potential in the world but without focus, your abilities and talents are often redundant. It is like being the world's best archer but without a target.

Thirdly, they sustain momentum. We have all set New Year's resolutions, only to fail within a few weeks. Effective goal setting, by breaking goals into bite-size chunks, creates mini-goals that are completed regularly and provide a regular sense of reward; an essential component in creating automatic habits. Seeing progress is addicting, literally, because of the dopamine released in your brain after attaining it. It is what the chimp craves. Just as a snowball grows in size as it rolls down a hill, momentum works in a similar way. Just think of the last time you were really "in the groove" where you said to yourself, "I'm on a roll!" That's momentum. Whatever you were doing you probably didn't want to stop because the feeling of reward was so good. Seeing 10 lbs. fall off your body, your six-pack emerge, and people complimenting you provides a fix of dopamine that keeps you motivated. Here we are using the chimp, and his urge for immediate satisfaction, to our advantage, as opposed to fighting against it.

With that being said, how does one successfully plan and implement goals? I have developed a method, which I refer to as "The System", to both plan meaningful goals and break them down in such a way as to maximize the likelihood of achieving them. "The System" has been with me for decades. It is the most logical, simple, and smartest way I have found to achieve whatever goals you set for yourself. This system is not a fancy or genius system, far from it, it is simple and logical, as it must be if you are to stick with it devotedly. I picked it up early in my career as a construction manager and it is a system engineers have been using to build large construction projects for centuries. If it can work for a billion-dollar underground subway network, it can work for you.

I was fortunate in my construction career to come across the very disciplined set of skills needed to build some extremely complex large-scale projects. From building an airport, nuclear power station, or a 5-mile-long bridge, the prospect of building such projects would send the inexperienced into a state of shock and overwhelm. Yet the process of planning these projects is fundamentally very simple and systematic. It has to be in order to break the complexities down to a level where they can be understood and implemented. Contrary to popular belief, an engineer's biggest skill lies not in sheer intelligence, but in his ability to break complex tasks into simpler ones.

The System uses a top-down organogram approach. I have provided a template sheet for the exact type of organogram I use for both construction management and for my goals. It is the same sort of system used to represent a company organization. The exact Microsoft Excel template I use can be downloaded for free at https://jason-strong.ck.page. For example, the boss resides at the top of the first tier, and all other tiers stem from this highest order tier. Underneath this first tier is a second tier, perhaps for the Vice Presidents. There are often multiple positions in this tier, perhaps three VPs who all report to the single first-tier boss. There will then be a third level for Project managers reporting to the second tier VPs. This tiered system continues all the way down to the lowest ranking member of the organization. There can be as many tiers as is necessary to completely break down the organization into its most fundamental components, with more complex organizations requiring more tiers and boxes.

The System mirrors this top-down breakdown for organization hierarchies and applies them to our goals using a three-tier approach. The first tier represents our ultimate goal. For construction, this will be our end goal, such as "build bridge". For our personal goals, it could be "achieve a weight of 150 lbs.", "stop smoking" or "sell 5000 products this year".

The second-tier breaks this first-tier into smaller components called projects. These projects are intermediary goals; they reduce high-level, but undetailed goals, into more detailed sub-goals. For example, "selling 5000 products this year" may be broken down into three projects: 1) Improve customer value of the product, 2) Create a marketing plan, and 3) Create a second product to sell. These three projects are not detailed enough in themselves to allow for an exact plan of action, but they break down the high-level first-tier goal in enough detail to start building actionable tasks.

From these projects can we build the third and final tier; tasks. This is the level where projects are broken up into small enough tasks where there is no room for interpretation and the course of action needed to achieve these tasks is precise and quantifiable. For example, the "create a marketing plan" project might be broken down into 1) Create a 30 second YouTube advertisement for the product and 2) Create a one-page magazine advertisement. These are precise and quantifiable tasks. The completion of both of these tasks will also complete your "create a marketing plan" project.

The likelihood of you actually following through on your goal stems from how effectively you define them in the first place. Writing goals on a piece of paper, to then be kept in your bedside table, will obviously never cut it. It must be a plan which is referred to continuously and updated as progress is made or direction is changed, just as how large construction projects are continuously monitored and modified by tracking the schedule. Failure to create clear cut goals will result in failure before you even start. Much like how profit is made when you buy, not when you sell, setting yourself up for success starts when you define your goals before they are even attempted.

Tier 1: Goals

So how does one effectively set goals which are likely to be achieved? There are three simple yet important questions that must be accurate and honestly answered to precisely define your goals. These are simply what, when, and why? The "what" component is self-explanatory. What exactly do you wish to achieve? Nail it down as precisely as possible and avoid using vague terms. Learning to play the piano is too vague; how will you know when you have "learned" it? Instead, I would define it as "play Clair de Lune by Debussy continuously with

10 or fewer mistakes". A finish line clear from any fog is essential to avoid overwhelm or procrastinating.

The "when" component is also straightforward yet difficult to accurately assess. With too little time you will find yourself failing, yet too much time will encourage procrastination. This period of time must also be short enough for you to be able to actively commit to your goals. Chances are slim you will be able to commit to a goal every day if the ultimate reward is 10 years away. Start by calculating as accurately as possible how long you think it will take to complete your goal, not just when you would like to achieve it. It has to be realistic and based on logic. This time period can, and should, be modified as you progress and the true scope of the goal becomes clearer.

Where most fail in creating committable goals is correctly and honestly identifying the "why" component. Why exactly is this goal so important to you? Many want to be financially independent by their forties. But why? Simply being financially independent does not provide you with any direct emotional benefit. Maybe the core reason is that you want to spend more time with family? Perhaps you want to start your own business to sell that product or service you always dreamed of? These are emotional drivers. To deduce the true emotional drivers for wanting to complete specific goals, I utilize another tool from my construction career; root cause analysis.

Whenever an accident occurs on a construction site, an effort is made to identify the root cause of the accident in order to stand the best chance of preventing the issue occurring in the future. For example, the immediate cause of falling off a ladder may be that the worker leaned too far over the side causing the ladder to topple. The initial lesson learned may be to not lean on a ladder and to instead come down and move the ladder to where you need to reach. Seems pretty straightforward but this won't necessarily stop others from falling off in the future. Instead, we perform a root cause analysis to determine the fundamental reason why the incident happened in order to completely prevent it from occurring again. We do this by simply asking "why?" three times. 1) Why did the worker fall? Because he leaned too far to the side? 2) Why did he lean too much? Because there is no space for the ladder underneath where the worker needs to work. 3) Why is there no space? Because someone has stockpiled timber where the worker needs to access. Here we have found the fundamental reason; materials are stockpiled on-site where people need to work. Instead of blaming the accident solely on the worker, the core reason is poor housekeeping on site. By addressing the true root cause of the incident, poor housekeeping, we can prevent the need for the worker to lean on the ladder altogether.

The same root cause analysis can be applied to determine the root emotional driver of your goals. You will know when you have delved deep enough and nailed this root cause as the thought of it will initiate a rush of emotions and dopamine from visualizing yourself in this position. For example, a personal goal for me is to run a marathon at age 60. This, in itself, is not a motivating goal, in fact, it is the complete opposite. I am not a running fanatic and the thought of putting myself through this terrifies me. I don't believe I would be able to achieve this goal with this reasoning alone. Using root cause analysis, however, I can start to find my emotional connection. 1)

Why do I want to run a marathon? Because I want to remain healthy in my later years. 2) Why do you want to remain healthy? Because I don't want to follow in the footsteps of my grandparents. 3) Why not? Because I do not want my family to worry about my health as I did my family's. Boom. That root cause instigated an extremely strong emotional connection as I have always had to worry about the poor health of my family. There is the real root cause. This is the fundamental emotional reason behind my goal and what I will draw upon in moments of weakness and doubt. Whether it be forcing myself to run on those particularly cold days or pushing through "the wall" during the marathon itself when my chimp inevitably asks me "why are you doing this?", I will have a strong emotional response on hand; "so my family does not have to endure the constant worry about my health that I had to with my elders".

To quickly recap, precisely define your goals by answering these three main questions: what, why, and when? Whilst the "what" and "when" components are quantifiable, the "why" component is emotional. Use root cause analysis to deduce the fundamental emotional driver of your goal by asking "why?" three times. If you cannot draw upon or conjure any feelings of strong emotion when visualizing your success, I dare say that goal is not truly important to you. Perhaps it is something others are pushing onto you; maybe your parents are encouraging you to get into medical school when you truly want to become a musician. If the emotional driver behind becoming a doctor isn't there, you will find it both very difficult and unrewarding to chase this goal and are more likely to fail. You will find better chances of success chasing the dream of becoming a musician, perhaps not financially, but in terms of feelings of accomplishment and fulfillment when it aligns with your fundamental emotional drivers.

As a final note on goals, goal setting is a process that changes over time. The goals you set in your twenties will most likely be very different from the goals you set in your forties. If your goals change and you no longer feel an emotional drive from them, that is ok. It is far better to switch to a new goal which means something to you emotionally than to waste time chasing one which doesn't. It is also good to have multiple goals. No matter how driven you are by your goals, sometimes you can burn out on tough, repetitive, or strenuous tasks. Shifting focus onto another goal is a good way to maintain progress and confidence without having to fight your chimp so hard. You can then come back to this particularly tough goal once refreshed.

Tier 2: Projects

Once your goal, with its root emotional driver, is precisely defined, the next step is to break this seemingly overwhelming goal into manageable pieces. The second tier splits the goal into multiple "projects". A goal of losing 50 lbs. in 20 weeks, for example, could be broken down into two constituent projects: 1) stick to a predetermined diet plan and 2) stick to a predetermined exercise routine. The aim of projects is to reduce an unquantifiable and emotional goal into small enough components where we can then start to plan individual and actionable tasks.

The number of projects needed to sufficiently break down a goal depends on the scope of the goal. Projects are medium-term sub-goals, perhaps of the timeline of a week to a month. They form the middle ground between emotional visualizations, as goals are, into actionable chunks of work which can then be broken down further into single actionable tasks. You can, and should, work on multiple projects at a time. For example, losing weight requires sticking to both diet and exercise projects simultaneously. Once all projects are complete, so too will be your top tier goal.

Tier 3: Tasks

The third and final tier, tasks, is where the magic happens. Tasks are the most basic level on the organogram and further break down projects into small enough single items where the whole scope of work is easily visualized. Each chunk represents a single actionable task that can be attempted immediately. In construction, we would continue breaking down projects into sufficiently small enough tasks where labor, materials, and equipment (such as excavators and laborers) can be accurately assigned, and hence the total time and cost of the project can be calculated. It is the combination of these small but quantifiable pieces of work that allow us to accurately piece together the entire project from start to finish.

Tasks must be actionable, i.e. physical and visible. This usually means allocating three key attributes to them; what, when, and how. For example, "read through quarterly reports" is too vague and should be turned into: "extract key financial data (the what) by reading through all four weekly reports (the how) and collate into a presentation from 1 p.m. to 5 p.m. (the when). When everything is laid out like this, there is little opportunity for overwhelm to instigate the chimp.

When you can see exactly what needs to be done to get from point A to point B, the task becomes a systematic process as opposed to a thinking exercise. This is perfect for the chimp who avoids the discomfort of overwhelm and confusion at all costs. Tasks should also be short in nature where possible, preferably a day, for a sense of immediate reward having achieved it, thereby satisfying the chimp and continuously reinforcing a positive habit loop.

Once your tasks are concisely actionable, they should be reviewed for feasibility. It may be too much to read all four reports in just four hours, so split it into two actionable tasks: 1) read through the first two weekly reports, extract key financial data, and collate into a presentation from 1 p.m. to 5 p.m. The next day you could then have a second task to read through the last two weekly reports, extract key financial data, and collate into a presentation from 9 a.m. to 1 p.m. Your tasks would ideally be achievable in one day or one sitting. Delaying the reward from completing tasks will decrease your enthusiasm and make the habit much harder to build.

The key to successful task-setting lies in ensuring that it contains one, and only one, actionable task. If the task is "call everyone on the list about the change of wedding date" this is more of a goal or project and needs to be broken down into one single actionable task (what, how, when). "Call (the how) John, Mary, Kevin, Jason and Julian to inform them of the new wedding date (the what) between 1 p.m. and 2 p.m. (the when). This may sound silly, but "call everyone" is too vague and requires extra thinking which risks involving the procrastination prone chimp. It is also more difficult to work out to any degree of accuracy how long the task will take. The more explicitly the task is set, the more likely it is to be completed. If the task has multiple components as the first one did i.e. create a list of people to call and call them, move it up to a project and break it down into single tasks.

Creating your "system" is one half of the equation, sticking to it religiously is another. Your tasks should be written down and carried with you everywhere you go. I use a daily planner as mentioned in the following chapter to ensure I actively work on them throughout the day. The bulk of goal setting will be performed in a single sitting where you define your goals as described above, break it down into projects, and then further into daily tasks. Once a week (Sunday) I have a calendar reminder set to review my system. Here I will delete tasks and projects which I have completed the previous week and transfer new tasks into my journal which are to be completed in the next week. As you progress towards your goals by completing their associated projects and tasks, your system might change as you realize what is and isn't working. But every Sunday, I set my next weeks' worth of tasks, update my system, and spend the next week attacking my tasks. This simple and systematic process is how strong habits become ingrained and goals are seen through to completion. The weekly review is absolutely critical to the system working and mustn't be ignored. Without it, you will lose your sense of progress and direction.

Task:

Download my organogram, or find your own, and build your own system. First, precisely define your goal. Ask yourself the three main questions: what, when, and why. For the "what" and "when" components, be as precise as possible. For the "why", use a root cause analysis and ask yourself exactly why you want to complete this goal at least three times. Keep going until you dig deep enough and find your fundamental emotional drive.

Now that you have precisely defined your emotionally driven goal, break it down into projects. Try to encompass all broad aspects that will be needed to achieve your goal. Remember projects are middlemen, they are the fundamental components of your goal that, when achieved together, must result in the completion of your goal.

Your projects allow you to start to visualize how your goal will be completed. Break these projects down further into actionable tasks. These tasks are single and quantitative items that can be tackled immediately. Ensure each task is defined in terms of what, how, and when.

Set a calendar alarm once a week to tick off completed tasks and projects and transfer next week's tasks into your journal. Update your system as and when you need to ensure it remains up to date and relevant.

Above all, make sure that as you change, your goals still remain relevant. If you find yourself procrastinating or hitting a plateau, readdress your emotional attachment to the goal. If it is still relevant to you, you will be revitalized by this emotional reminder. If not, you may have outgrown your original goal. Either way, you are still continually progressing towards a life aligned to your values.

1.5 Get Yourself A Little Black Book

With so much going on in life, from building a career to taking care of family, it is no wonder our days often feel overwhelming and out of control. Without a methodical plan many end up bouncing between spontaneous tasks with little thought to efficiency or time management, often resulting in very busy yet unproductive days. Combine a busy life with a terrible memory, like mine, and you have the perfect storm for spending a lot of time achieving very little.

One simple tool to help bring order to our precious few waking hours is to plan all daily activities and events in a daily notepad/journal. I call mine the "little black book" because I buy my journals as small as possible, preferably A6 or A7 size, ensuring I have no excuse to not keep it in my pocket at all times. While journals and planners are not a new concept, many use them as simple to-do lists as opposed to methodically planning and prioritizing goals. It is a tip I observed from a wealthy friend, who told me how he could never run his complex business without his "little black book" to ensure he remained focused on the tasks that are most important. I have used it daily for most of my adult life without fail and I attribute its careful and strategic use to much of my productivity. Without it, I would almost certainly work twice as hard while achieving far less. It allows one to work smarter as opposed to working harder.

It is not just my wealthy friend who religiously lives by this little black book. Sir Richard Branson, founder of the Virgin Group, and arguably one of the most celebrated entrepreneurs of our time, is also a known pocket journal advocate. When asked about items he takes wherever he goes, Branson singled out one item as being most important. In a 2006 interview, he said: "It may sound ridiculous, but my most important item is the little notebook I always carry in my back pocket. I think the number one thing that I take with me when I'm traveling is this notebook. I could never have built the Virgin Group into the size it is without those few bits of paper."

Branson elaborated on his note-taking habits on his personal blog. He said, "If you have a thought but don't write it down, by the next morning it may be gone forever." Once, when Branson had an idea for a business metaphor, he didn't have a notebook nearby. So, he just scribbled the thought down in his passport. It worked. But he would have preferred a notebook.

Greek shipping magnate and billionaire Aristotle Onassis once gave an interview in which he shared his "million-dollar lesson": "Always carry a notebook. Write everything down. When you have an idea, write it down. When you meet someone new, write down everything you know about them. That way, you will know how much time they are worth. When you hear something interesting, write it down. Writing it down will make you act upon it. If you don't write it down you will forget it. That is a million-dollar lesson they don't teach you in business school!" Mark Twain, George Patton, Thomas Jefferson, Charles Darwin, George Lucas, Ernest Hemingway, Ludwig van Beethoven, Ben Franklin, Thomas Edison, Leonardo da Vinci, Frank Capra, and John Rockefeller, some of the most successful people of all time, are all known for their regular use of journals.

The primary purpose of this notebook is to minimize the amount of stress and anxiety induced through overwhelm. Organizing thoughts and tasks clarifies what needs to be done and helps avoid procrastinating or being distracted by tasks that yield the least benefit. The act of planning your day in full and freeing your mind from the barrage of thoughts swirling around, is extremely therapeutic. All your problems, and how you will overcome them, are now clarified in front of you; when the end-goal is in sight we are much more motivated to accomplish it.

There are three main ways this little black book can add significant value to your life. The first is in providing immediate access to what I call a "thought dump". This thought dump is simply where any thoughts or tasks that spontaneously pop into your mind are immediately noted for future reference. Say you suddenly remember you need to buy baby formula or need to call your significant other to remind them that the internet bill needs to be paid, but are too busy to address these issues at that specific moment, these thoughts should be immediately noted before you have a chance to forget them. The note should also be so simple that it can be written in just a few seconds, allowing you to temporarily remove it from your mind until you have time to address it fully. Instead of wasting focus trying to remember the task throughout the day, this thought dump allows you to remove it from your mind and free up mental resources for more important tasks, whilst also decluttering your mind and reducing the mind fog induced through overwhelm.

This thought dump section of your notepad should then be reviewed later when you can dedicate more time to developing the thought of turning it into an actionable task. Remember the point of this thought dump is to make a quick note of something important you later need to address, without having to dedicate any extra time or effort trying to address it in the moment. When in a meeting, and an important thought springs to mind, there is a good chance you will have forgotten it by the end of the meeting. Just a simple note made in a few seconds will be enough to prompt your memory later when you have more time to come back and address it fully. I think of this thought dump as an external hard drive for my brain, freeing some much-needed brainpower for more pressing tasks.

The second benefit of this little black book lies in organizing your tasks, derived from breaking down your goals through "The System" as described in the previous chapter. Once a week your master goal-setting document should be reviewed and updated to remove completed tasks and projects and transfer new ones to your planner for the upcoming week. These tasks should be written in your pocket journal for each respective day to ensure your days are structured and focused around completing these concise goals. If these goals are not written down, nor crossed off once completed, there is little accountability for failing to complete them. It is too easy to procrastinate on a task when there is no commitment towards completing it. By writing tasks in your journal, you make a written commitment to yourself to complete these tasks within the day, and by failing to complete them upon review each night, you are held accountable for the failure to complete them. This may appear harsh, but this accountability is essential in committing to our goals.

By planning daily schedules in advance, we provide a real sense of structure focused around productively completing our goals. This was a significant contributor in helping me clear the overwhelm that clouded my judgment. It also decluttered my mind and enabled me to sleep much easier. For those who have trouble sleeping during busy and stressful points in their careers or everyday lives, the structure provided through this simple daily planner can be an excellent tool in combating an overactive mind.

The third key benefit of this little black book lies in productively prioritizing your tasks to ensure your time is utilized as effectively as possible. Ideally, you should focus on tasks that return the greatest investment for the time committed. Time is constant; we only have a limited amount of time in the day which we can dedicate towards completing tasks. But the value derived from different tasks varies. Don't dedicate an hour to admin work when you have the potential to close a large deal with a new client. It can be tempting to postpone difficult work, such as trying to sell to a new client, in favor of easier work, such as filling out your expense reports. Remember the chimp seeks the path of least resistance at all times. Both tasks may be essential, but their return on time invested will be different. The tasks you set in your planner should be filtered based on returned value and importance, whether this is financial or any other form of value. Rank all daily tasks in your planner, with the number 1 task being of the greatest importance. The highest priority tasks should be solely focused on first, continuing with other tasks in order of their respective ranking once higher priority tasks are completed.

Although it can be alarming when writing out the myriad of daily tasks that need to be completed, it is a necessary first step to enforce order amongst potential chaos. The real value comes from this prioritization of tasks, however. The Pareto principle (also known as the 80/20 rule) states that, for many events, roughly 80 percent of results come from just 20 percent of your time. Just 20 percent of those tasks on your to-do list will provide 80 percent of your progress. Conversely, 80 percent of your tasks will result in a mere 20 percent of results (i.e. you spent a lot of time achieving very little). Writing your tasks out in the little black books helps you assess which of your tasks you need to prioritize, maximizing productivity whilst minimizing time expended. If you have more tasks on your list than hours in the day, you can clearly see what tasks are of lesser value and need to be pushed to tomorrow.

This notepad should be with you at all times during the day. Whether it be in your pocket or bag, it needs to be close at hand to immediately note any thoughts for future reference and ensure you focus your time towards your highest priority tasks. Regularly crossing off completed tasks also provides a much-needed morale boost as the day ticks away. Whereas many start to flag around 3 p.m., I am still highly focused knowing I am not too far from completing my daily tasks.

I have tried using apps and electronic notes in a bid to keep up with modern trends. Although writing notes on a phone is much more convenient, I found myself not able to stick to it as consistently. This may differ for you, but the process of physically writing tasks with pen and paper seems to be much more engaging. It creates a binding commitment to myself. The process of actively crossing them off your list once completed is also much more rewarding when trying to build habits.

Again, this little black book will become the single point of organization in your life. It is imperative to keep it on you at all times, both for a reminder of your highest priority tasks and for taking down notes on the fly, freeing up limited mental resources for higher-value tasks. This is why my diary is extremely small, just A6 size. Even A7 can be just as practical. I always keep it in my pocket alongside my phone, ensuring I never go anywhere without it. I am rarely more than an arm's length away from it, except for the hour or so when I exercise.

Of course, taking notes won't matter if you don't follow through. Use your notes to develop ideas, problem-solve, and create goals. Branson points out that Virgin Atlantic's success is in the small details, which means nothing can be forgotten or delayed.

Task:

Buy a small notepad! Transfer the most important tasks from your goal setting document and allocate them to respective days for the upcoming week. Rank them in terms of priority, with the number 1 being the task of highest priority, with the 80:20 rule in mind, making sure that 20 percent of most important tasks are ranked above all others. If there doesn't seem to be enough time to complete all your tasks, move the lowest ranking tasks to the next day. Sometimes you will be genuinely overwhelmed with too many tasks to do in too little time. Don't stress, this is beyond your control. What is in your control, however, is prioritizing those which are most important to make the best use of the time you do have.

1.6 Willpower is a Limited Resource

Willpower is a vague and misunderstood trait that is often misused and rarely applied productively. In 2011, 27 percent of respondents from the Stress in America survey reported that a lack of willpower presented the greatest barrier to change. But it is not a lack of willpower that is the problem. Rather it is the misuse in situations where it is neither productive nor justified that is.

Defined as the "control exerted to do something or restrain impulses", willpower is usually thought of as that extra bit of effort found deep within the mind to push through moments where the temptation to quit is overwhelming. Athletes draw upon willpower to pick up the pace in the final mile of a marathon when their bodies are screaming for them to stop. Others call upon it to avoid eating those last few cookies. Whatever the situation, willpower can yield extreme strength in moments of dire weakness. Unfortunately, willpower cannot always be relied upon consistently. Sometimes the temptation to give in is too great even for the strongest of wills.

Many argue that willpower is a finite resource. The notion of "ego depletion" refers to the idea that self-control or willpower draws upon a limited pool of mental resources that can be expended and once you run out of energy, you're more likely to lose self-control. Others have tried to debunk this myth by arguing that willpower is only limited because they have been told it is. My experience, however, has led me to the belief that willpower, as a tool, lies somewhere in the middle of these.

Willpower, in the right circumstance, can be an incredibly powerful tool capable of pushing humans to extremes we might not even have thought possible. An athlete, for example, is the perfect demonstrator of the sheer mental strength willpower can summon. A marathon runner, in the last few miles of a grueling 26-mile run, will at some point hit a mental wall where every fiber in their body urges them to stop. Their oxygen-deprived muscles cramp and their chimp tries everything in its power to stop the runner from taking one more step. Yet the runner, recalling the past year of pain they have had to endure in training, digs deep and finds a burst of adrenaline and dopamine to do whatever it takes to get themselves across the line. With the mind sharpened and their focus narrowed, both brain and body are focused solely on keeping one foot moving in front of the other. This is where willpower should be called upon; in these last ditched, short-lived do-or-die moments driven by raw emotion.

Did the runner rely upon this same force of willpower every time they trained, however? Absolutely not. There are very few people who could wake up at 5 a.m. in the freezing, pouring rain and force their mind and body to the edge of its limit every day, whilst constantly fighting the urge to stop. Instead, their training schedule is methodically planned, and incrementally progressed. It may start from a one-mile jog every other day up. The following week increases this to two miles as the mind and body adjust. Gradually, they adapt to a rigorous training schedule that is based upon habits and incremental progress as opposed to brute force use of willpower every training session. An athlete understands that willpower is a powerful resource that should be used sparingly.

If willpower is neither finite nor infinite, then it is instead limited. Willpower can be thought of as having a cooldown period where the body and mind need to recover from the trauma in order to recharge. Like a race car, the harder you rev the engine the more fuel it uses. Willpower consumes this "mental fuel" extremely quickly and is therefore susceptible to fatiguing quicker. You may be able to push yourself to the extreme physical limit on one day, but doing it again the next will not be so easy. The more "mental fuel" that's consumed, the greater the fatigue and the longer the recharge time needed to recover.

Smokers are an excellent example of well-intentioned yet misguided use of willpower. Attempting to stop by going "cold turkey" is far more mentally taxing than gradually cutting down incrementally. You may be able to avoid smoking altogether for those first few days using sheer willpower alone, but after a week or so the mind will fatigue and your mental energy levels drop dramatically. There has not been enough time for your mind to recover and recharge from the constant use of willpower. This is why only five percent of smokers are able to quit cold turkey. Taking an incremental approach, however, combined with the use of medications, has been shown to improve quit rates by 50 to 70 percent. The greater use of habits, as we see later, as opposed to sheer willpower alone, allows for a more reliable source of sustainable long-term mental energy.

Willpower, therefore, is best used short-term for those moments where a short sharp burst of adrenaline is needed, provided there has been enough time to enable the mind to rest and recharge from previous use. Longer-term use of willpower, however, is not sustainable; instead, we need to build habits. Willpower and good habits complement each other perfectly and efficient application of each in its correct context is what enables both long- and short-term commitment to our goals. The world's best athletes and most successful businessmen do not necessarily possess greater willpower than the average man, they have simply built better habits and understand when to rely on habits and when to call upon willpower. This elite tier understands that relying on lifestyle changes and habits is a far more effective long-term strategy, whereas utilizing self-control and willpower should be reserved for special situations and used sparingly.

Habits are more reliable long-term because they take the emotion out of the task at hand and instead, transfer it to the more automatic part of the brain, the prefrontal cortex. Take skipping breakfast, for example. Those who have grown up always eating breakfast, or have done it for a long time, do not think twice about preparing breakfast every morning. It is a habit ingrained over years of repetition. It becomes an automatic task that we perform on autopilot. Yet for those who haven't built this habit, it becomes all too easy to skip the meal entirely. It takes active mental energy to dedicate time to make it and thus is often skipped. It is our emotions, such as fear and overwhelm, that encourage the limbic system to give up. By eliminating this aspect as far as possible, and instead relying on the automatic part of the brain, we avoid the greatest source of failure altogether.

In 2015, psychologists Brian Galla and Angela Duckworth published a paper in the Journal of Personality and Social Psychology, finding across six studies and more than 2,000 participants that people who are good at self-control also tend to have good habits — like exercising regularly, eating healthily, sleeping well, and studying.

"People who are good at self-control seem to be structuring their lives in a way to avoid having to make a self-control decision in the first place," Galla explains. And structuring your life is a skill. People who do the same activity, like running or meditating, at the same time every day have an easier time accomplishing their goals, not because of their greater willpower, but because the routine makes it easier. Those who appear to have greater willpower are instead most likely relying on habits built over many years.

The key takeaway here is understanding the different roles willpower and habits play in achieving goals. Willpower is an incredibly powerful tool for immediate bursts of mental energy. It is quick to act and extremely motivating but offset by the time it needs to "recharge", and cannot, therefore, be relied upon long term. Habits, on the other hand, are the yin to willpower's yang. Although they can take months or years to develop and are not as motivating in the heat of the moment, they allow for reliable commitment towards goals by taking the negative emotion away from activities. For those who wish to finally stick to that diet that has been eluding them for so long, first build gradual habits, such as a better diet and exercise where progress is incremental so as to avoid the initial overwhelm stemming from new and uncomfortable tasks. Once these habits start to become automatic, so too will the results. You may still have to rely on willpower to get you through those particularly tough times; perhaps a bad day at work urges you to demolish that tub of ice cream, but your habits will soon kick back in whilst your willpower recharges. It is this appropriate use of both willpower and habits that, when used in synergy, turn man into a highly productive machine.

Task:

It is imperative we understand when to rely upon willpower and when to rely upon habits. Look at the goals or moments in your life where you failed previously. Failure was most likely the result of a moment of weakness that discouraged and prevented you from further attempts. Think about how you could have transferred some of the tasks away from relying on willpower alone and how you could have first crafted them into habits.

Apply this to either your current or future goals. Identify the largest sources of potential failure when you are most likely to give up and find a way to instead craft them into habits. For example, those who wish to start running for 30 minutes every evening, but are struggling with motivation after just a few days, scale it back and focus on first building the habit. Perhaps simply go for a 15-minute walk at the same time every evening to first build the habit of routinely performing this task at the same time every day. After a couple of weeks, the urge to leave the house and take that walk will become increasingly more automatic; soon you won't even have to think about it. Incrementally build this habit from here; either increase your walking time or pick up the pace. Save willpower for those particularly cold or rainy evenings to which it is best suited.

1.7 Prepare for Tomorrow Today

A productive day starts the night before. A little planning in the evening ensures you start the following morning as productively as possible by organizing your thoughts and actions whilst minimizing time spent fumbling around in the morning while half asleep. For those who wish to wake early, perhaps to sneak a quick workout in before work, preparing the essentials the night before makes those early starts much more manageable. When the alarm starts shrieking at 5 a.m. on a cold winter morning, the temptation to hit snooze is often inescapable. But knowing everything you need for the day is already in place may provide just enough encouragement to help overcome this early morning dread.

Firstly, set out everything you possibly can the evening before. Work clothes should be laid out before bed so no time is wasted trying to pick out whatever ensemble just about passes as presentable. The same goes for those early gym-goers; pack your gym bag in its entirety and leave it next to the door. Place your keys and wallet in a known place to avoid frantically searching for them in the morning. There is no worse start to a day than spending the morning rushing around the house like a headless chicken to then arrive late to work. Not only will you have lost valuable time, but the frustration will stick with you for hours, souring your mood. All before you even start your working day.

Breakfast, the most important meal of the day, should also be prepared as much as possible the night before. Place your cereal and spoon in a bowl ready to just add milk in the morning. You are much less likely to skip breakfast when it's laid out right in front of you, and whether you are on a diet or not, breakfast is the most important meal of the day to provide the energy needed to jump-start your productivity. I start every morning off with a shake of some kind. I place all my fruits, nuts, and seeds in a blending cup and place them in the fridge. In the morning, all I need to do is add water and blend; a quick, easy, and nutritious way to build early morning energy.

Secondly, do all cleaning, tidying, and washing up the night before. Waking up to a sink full of smelly dishes and clutter all over the house will lead to a cluttered mental state. Conversely, waking up to a clean and orderly house creates a feeling of control and starts the day with a more positive outlook. It may sound silly but the subconscious is extremely influential. The time invested cleaning is the same regardless of whether it's performed in the evening or morning, but doing it in the evening can help start your day more positively. It's a no brainer.

Thirdly, I highly recommend preparing your meals for the week in advance. Firstly, cooking in large batches saves time compared to cooking multiple individual meals every day. Every Sunday I go through the effort of preparing simple, nutritious, cheap, yet tasty food for the whole week. This sounds tedious but the investment of time on a Sunday evening is only a couple of hours, much less than that which would be expended cooking meals individually throughout the entire week. A week's worth of overnight oats for breakfast can be made in just 10 minutes. A tasty three-bean chili cooked in just 30 minutes provides me with an effortless lunch every day. Even my dinners are prepared in tubs so I can simply place them in the microwave for a couple of minutes. This might not be for everyone, especially for those who enjoy the practice of cooking, but for those who struggle to eat well, or even at all, or simply wish to free up more time, it can be a highly productive tool.

Meal prepping is essential for those seeking a healthier diet. Not only can they be nutritious, but more importantly they reduce the temptation to binge on unhealthy foods. Fast food is named as such for its extreme convenience. These places rely on your inability to prepare food in advance. The same temptations are avoided when returning home from a long and stressful day at work. You are hungry, had a crap day, worried about making ends meet and what do you do? Spend the next 30 mins preparing something healthy or grab chips and a soda and collapse on the sofa? What about if you had a tasty meal already prepared in the fridge, where all you had to do was pop it in the microwave for just a couple of minutes? You are much less likely to go for damaging foods knowing you are two easy minutes away from a delicious fulfilling meal.

The fourth and final essential pre-sleep check is to evaluate your daily tasks as planned from your goal setting exercise. This takes the form of two parts: evaluating the day's performance and preparing the next day's activities. Crossing off your tasks for the day is extremely rewarding and eliminates much of the anxiety about work or your personal life that keeps many awake at night.

Similarly, setting the following days tasks helps clear the mind of overwhelm and allows for a worry-free night's sleep. I used to suffer mildly from anxiety when sleeping, especially in my younger years when my career was more stressful. Many valuable hours of much-needed sleep were lost due to tossing and turning and wondering about the things I had to do the next day. The simple act of writing my tasks for the next day the evening before, however, instantly decluttered the mind, enabling me to finally sleep like a baby. Even on holiday, when I feel I should be escaping the everyday tasks of life, I feel I still must set myself some tasks or else the day would be wasted. These tasks can be relaxing too, such as eating at restaurant x, which was recommended as a must-eat restaurant, or seeing x and y attractions. It enables me to feel as if I'm making the most of my limited holiday time by providing structure. Furthermore, waking up knowing your plan of attack for the entire day helps you rise with a little more enthusiasm, whilst also avoiding that dreaded procrastination.

By setting tasks and planning the following day the night before, I can walk into my office the next day knowing exactly what I need to do and how I need to go about doing it. I already know which of my tasks are the greatest priority and need to be tackled first. This avoids the dreaded Monday blues; I'm sure many of you know the feeling of starting your Monday morning distracted by social media whilst trying to avoid the frustration of picking back up where you left off last Friday. By preparing your day the night before, you can turn that dreaded morning rush into a relaxing build-up to a highly productive day.

Task:

Make a simple to-do list of all the tasks you could do the evening before to make your morning as effortless as possible. This may include laying out your clothes, packing your gym bag, cleaning your house, and making your breakfast. Anything which you will have to do in the morning, see if you can find a way to prepare it the night before. Remember the time invested to do this is the same whether it be done at night or in the morning. Yet it is far more productive to do these things when you're too tired to do anything productive at night as opposed to stressing yourself out in the morning.

1.8 Create a Functional Sleep Pattern

Six, eight, ten, twelve. These are all the supposed minimum hours of sleep I have heard experts declare necessary over the years. The amount of sleep, however, is only half the equation in creating an efficient sleeping pattern. Sleep should also be timed to maximize your most productive hours during the day.

Mariah Carey claims she needs 15 hours of sleep a night along with 20 dehumidifiers. Jim Cramer, the host of CNBC's Mad Money, claims he needs just four hours of sleep between 11:30 p.m. and 3:45 a.m. to feel well-rested and alert, whilst rarely needing an alarm to rise. Cramer's not the only one. Notable leaders such as Theranos CEO Elizabeth Holmes, Yahoo CEO Marissa Mayer, and even ex-US President Barack Obama rarely, if ever, get what's considered a full night's sleep. Yet these people still thrive.

How much sleep you need is not determined by how lazy you may be or how able you are to force yourself out of bed. Whilst the scientific theory behind why, and for how long, humans must sleep is still not exactly known, the consensus suggests that the brain needs sleep to perform housekeeping and general maintenance duties, since it doesn't get much recovery time during the day. While we sleep, the brain repairs cellular damage, removes toxins that accumulate during the day, and builds neural networks and habits from the day's experiences.

Research from the University of California, San Francisco, investigated how a lady who slept for just four hours a night was able to function normally in comparison to the majority of the population who usually require double that amount. Ying-Hui Fu and her colleagues compared the genome of different family members. They discovered a tiny mutation in a gene called DEC2 that was present in those who were short-sleepers, but not in members of the family who required a more normal length of sleep, nor in the 250 unrelated volunteers. When the team bred mice to simulate this same gene mutation, the rodents were also found to sleep less whilst functioning as competently as regular mice when given physical and cognitive tasks. This suggests that short-sleepers are genetically predisposed to need less sleep, presumably because their brains can perform the necessary maintenance quicker. It is estimated that just 1 percent of the population is capable of short-sleeping.

This leads to a major insight; the amount of sleep required depends not only on external factors, such as how active you are throughout the day but also on genetics. It is therefore not accurate to base your sleep patterns on other peoples'. You should have a good indication of how much sleep you require to function effectively throughout the day. Most sources suggest that the average is around eight hours per night.

I have known of a few entrepreneurs, high-level managers, and CEOs, who purposely sacrifice sleeping hours to work earlier and longer. As well-intentioned as this is, however, it is counterproductive. One of the main purposes of sleep is to process what we have learned throughout the day.

Before the 1950s, it was commonly believed that sleep was a passive activity during which the body and brain were dormant. But it turns out that sleep is a period where the brain engages in several activities vital to learning.

One such activity revolves around "brain plasticity," or the brain's ability to learn from stimulus. Brain plasticity enables the brain to rewire itself and create new neural pathways based on the experiences and memories encountered throughout the day. If you spend the day learning to ride a bike, for example, the following sleep will see new neural pathways created, making the process of riding a bike more efficient. Too little sleep prevents this learning mechanism from fully building, hindering progress, and increasing the total amount of time required to learn. This brain plasticity mechanism is also how consistent and repetitive tasks are incrementally crafted into habits.

Although there is no exact best time for sleeping (eight hours of sleep is still eight hours of sleep), we should generally seek to synchronize when we sleep with our body's natural clock. Humans are naturally predisposed to sleep with the movements of the sun and have an inherent sleeping function called a biological clock, an innate mechanism that controls the physiological activities of an organism which change on a daily, seasonal, yearly, or other regular cycles. This mechanism is responsible for circadian rhythms, a natural, internal process that regulates the sleep-wake cycle and repeats every 24 hours. This cycle is responsible for man's need to sleep and wake as the sun rises and falls. This is why it is far easier to wake at 6 a.m. in the summer when it is light as opposed to the same time in winter when it is still dark. Unfortunately, with modern work schedules, it is not always possible to rise and fall with the sun, but we should at least try to minimize the negative effects of waking outside these times as much as possible. Staying up into the early hours of the morning and then sleeping in till midday, for example, does not sync well with our internal clocks.

Also conspiring against our sleep patterns is the fact that human intelligence has surpassed the body's ability to adapt. Whilst the advent of alarm clocks now allows us to physically break these natural circadian rhythms, we cannot as easily break them biologically. Anyone who has worked extended night shifts knows the toll night shifts can subconsciously take on the body, including stomach upsets and the feeling of being a "zombie" (someone who suffers from memory loss, confusion, and irritability). Having worked in the construction industry for many years, I can personally attest to the effects even consistent night shift sleeping patterns can take on the body.

One way to minimize the effects of falling out of sync with our biological clocks is to ensure our sleeping patterns are kept as consistent as possible. That means waking and sleeping at the same time every day. The body, and its evolutionary instinct to maximize efficiency, will seek to become as efficient as possible in the time you are awake when it knows what sleeping pattern it can expect. You will find your waking hours much more productive when you wake and sleep at the same time every day as opposed to sleeping at varying times where your body is kept guessing. Efficient sleep patterns are born out of strict habits and, like any other habit, require consistency and repetition to master.

So, we now know the importance of ensuring we get enough sleep and that we should synchronize it with our natural biological clocks as much as is practically possible. The only remaining question is whether there is a more efficient time for sleeping?

Optimum sleeping times vary between individuals and their different schedules, but there is one general rule that applies to all. The time you sleep should complement the hours during the day where you are most productive. For example, when I wake at 5 a.m. I am too tired to do anything that requires mental focus or creativity. So, I make the most of this time by exercising where cognitive demand is minor. Conversely, after exercise and a coffee at around 7 a.m., I am fully alert and ready to work. In the evenings, I tire significantly at around 7 p.m. Trying to accomplish anything mentally demanding past this point is inefficient as my productivity is halved and my work prone to errors. Between 7 p.m. and 9 p.m, I use this time to completely unwind, watch TV or YouTube and just generally do anything which I enjoy and which gives me a chance to relax. I can do this in good conscience having made the best use of my time prior and having accomplished all the daily tasks I set for myself. I then sleep between 9-9:30 p.m. ready to wake again at 5 a.m. This may be too early for some, but I take advantage of my prime work window between 7 a.m. and 7 p.m. (with regular breaks of course).

The first step in creating your functional sleep pattern, therefore, is to determine your most productive hours. I believe most people lie on a normal distribution curve where mental alertness starts at zero immediately after waking up, reaches a peak after a few hours, and then starts to slowly decline back towards zero as fatigue sets in. Many profess they are night owls who perform their best work late at night. Although I cannot reasonably claim to know how productive someone truly is having been awake for so long, I do believe that for most people their minds, and bodies, peak soon after waking and gradually decline throughout the day, similar to how the second half of a marathon is so much more demanding than the first half.

The biggest error I see others make (which I also used to be notorious for) is staying awake past the point where the body first hints it needs sleep. Many force themselves to stay awake past this point simply for the sake of staying awake. During my early twenties, I would stay up until midnight simply because I wanted to make the most of my free time. Having to dedicate most of the day to work can be distressing and leave little time to truly enjoy oneself. But because I was too tired to do anything productive past 7 p.m., I would essentially stay up and watch TV until I couldn't keep my eyes open anymore. To make matters worse, going to bed at midnight meant I slept in later. I would wake at 6 a.m. to the deafening roar of my alarm clock, having had far too little sleep, and rush to get to work on time. As a result, I often skipped breakfast and did not pack lunches, essentially ruining my day before it even started. Whilst the reasoning to maximize free time is understandable, when it means staying awake past the point of fatigue, it is highly inefficient in almost every way.

Instead, try sleeping when your body suggests it is ready to rest. And it will tell you if you listen to it; the body craves sleep as much as any other resource. By all means take an hour or so to wind down before sleeping to do those things you take pleasure from, but trade those pointless hours staying awake past the point where your eyes feel heavy for fresh productive hours in the morning where you can accomplish more work more productively. Despite sleeping earlier, one doesn't lose any time, it is simply trading unproductive late-night time for highly productive day time when your mind is fresh and rested.

I use the hours of 5 a.m. and 9 p.m. only as a point of reference to my routine. If you are fortunate enough to be able to start work later, and can therefore sleep later, optimize your situation. But we all have those closing few hours where we are too tired to do anything productive and would benefit from trading them for more productive hours once the mind is rested. Changing a sleep pattern will take some commitment (put it in your habit table for 50 days) but once the habit sticks, and you swap unproductive for productive time, you will benefit greatly with little compromise.

1.9 Work First, Play Later

Of all the bad habits to have, delaying work which could be done now is perhaps the most frustrating. We are all guilty of it to some degree, some worse than others. Whilst the saying "work first, play later" or "work hard, play hard" has been around since time immemorial, understanding how to successfully implement the habit by correctly balancing work and play through efficient application of the habit loop prevents most from ever achieving this zen-like habit.

To clarify, I am not suggesting to work longer and harder to achieve a greater quantity of work. What I am addressing, however, is how the balance between work and play can be made more productive. Many tend to have the balance tilted inefficiently. Two people who both perform five hours of work a day may be equally productive overall, but those who commit to completing their work earlier, and reward themselves once complete, succumb far less to stress than those who tend to put it off until the last minute, having spent their day first playing. That feeling of last-minute rush when your fatigued brain starts to shut down is never fun. But by committing to work when your mind is most receptive to it, both the quality and quantity will be superior, and the frustrations of procrastination avoided altogether. The problem is further exacerbated when work becomes linked to frustration; the more frequently you become frustrated with delaying work the more your chimp will associate the two, making you much less likely to start working altogether. On the other hand, when work is linked to a more productive and less stressful part of your day, the link between them will be more positive and procrastination less likely a result.

I do not blame people for procrastinating or think of them as lazy or lesser people. Remember that humans have an inherent inability to think long-term through the hunter-gatherer "only catch what you can carry" mentality. Being more intelligent than every other animal, however, allows us to consciously overcome this instinct through discipline instilled by habit building.

The benefits of a work first, play later mentality are numerous. Firstly, most people are more productive earlier on in the day when they are better rested and more willing to apply themselves. Anyone who has had to work late into the night knows that productivity is slashed dramatically when you're tired, where work tends to take longer and at a lesser quality. We make our life far harder than it needs to be by postponing work. I am aware that there are people who are convinced they are night owls, but I do wonder how one's brain can be sharper the longer it is used, much like how our bodies are far less capable in the second half of a marathon than in the first.

Contrast this with others who tend to postpone important work to fulfill their primal urges for instant gratification, i.e. they play first. We all suffer from time to time with procrastination, often caused by subconsciously avoiding something we don't want to do, either because we know it will be uncomfortable or because we do know exactly how to complete the task and cannot see the end goal; we are overwhelmed. The problem is this instant gratification offered by procrastination comes with strings attached; chiefly the guilt experience knowing that you should be doing something else. This often diminishes the quality of the reward, trapping yourself in a circle of frustration, and never being able to fully enjoy pleasure time. Not only are you frustrated having procrastinated all day, but you also cannot even enjoy the instant gratification procrastination supposedly offers because of the guilt of avoiding what you know you should be doing instead.

So how do we go about successfully building this elusive "work first, play later" mentality? By now I'm hoping you are starting to answer the question yourselves using the tools explained numerous times throughout this book. Relying on willpower and force of mind alone is not sustainable. Many try to set this very goal as a New Year's resolution and ultimately fail very quickly. Instead, we need to let the autopilot part of the brain do the hard work for us, and we do this by building habits.

The main tool we are going to use to successfully build this habit is through setting actionable tasks broken down from our goals (i.e. "The System" as described earlier). Each day we should set an appropriate number of tasks to be completed before the day's end. The skill here, that comes mainly through experience and practice, is in setting an appropriate number of tasks that are reasonably able to be completed in the limited hours available, without too much stress. We are aiming for consistency to build habits; too much work every day will require excessive amounts of willpower which is not sustainable. Once we have completed the day's tasks and crossed them from the list, can we then be free to relax and enjoy the rest of the day guilt-free? The real benefit here is the association your brain starts to make with working first to be rewarded with pleasure later.

Your chimp, always seeking comfort and pleasure, will eventually start subconsciously encouraging you to complete your tasks earlier as it recognizes that this is usually followed by pleasure.

It would be counterproductive, however, to try and accomplish every single task consecutively with no break or reward in between. This approach demands considerable willpower that is not sustainable, and there is no sense of reward to complete the habit loop. Instead, regular breaks with a sense of reward should be taken after accomplishing a set number of tasks or progress towards a particular task. For example, I might have just one daily task of writing a single chapter for a book, an activity that can take well over four hours to complete. I cannot possibly think logically and critically for this length of time, so I will take regular play breaks to reward my time committed. For example, I might work for 2 hours and take a 30-minute coffee break. The periods in which you should reward yourself will depend on your specific situation; completing a very mentally demanding task may require longer or more frequent breaks as you burn through mental focus quicker. Again, successful implementation of the work first, play later mentality requires an understanding of your work ability, and knowing how long you can apply yourself before needing a break.

Whilst the time in which you allow yourself to play is not set in stone, the mentality behind the work first play later theory still holds; you assign yourself a set time frame for work or complete a task and reward yourself with a guilt-free reward. Thus, the habit loop cycle completes and you become one iteration closer to turning willpower into habit. The reward isn't some gimmick that is supposed to give you a boost of willpower to push through your task, it is a very real science-based process that provides a small release of dopamine to strengthen the habit loop.

Do not make the mistake of rewarding yourself when you get bored, however. It can be tempting to switch focus when you are bored or starting to flag and convince yourself that boredom relates to progress. Rewards must be associated with a sense of tangible progress to build the habit, such as completing X tasks or performing Y hours of work. Rewarding yourself with a break just because you become bored with your task will not only avoid building a progress-based habit but, more dangerously, strengthen the habit of stopping when you become bored.

Now, when I talk about play, I'm talking in a broad sense about the things that bring you amusement, enjoyment, or relaxation and are considered fun and rewarding. They're the things you love to do, no strings attached. It doesn't have to be productive; it just needs to be something you enjoy enough to provide a strong enough incentive. For me, I have the guilty pleasure of watching copious amounts of YouTube videos. For others, it could be gardening, golfing, scrapbooking, baking, fishing, or sleeping. Anything goes.

Having completed my set tasks throughout the day, I can now rest easy with great peace of mind knowing my reward comes with no strings attached. My tasks are checked off, I have made progress towards my ultimate goals and I can now unload, enjoy myself, and sleep peacefully. Over time, this habit will allow for your brain to recognize that pleasure proceeds work, and will, therefore, encourage you to work to obtain this reward.

1.10 Progress Takes Time

I am an avid reader of biographies. I cannot recall the number of times I must have read the life accounts of Benjamin Franklin, John. D. Rockefeller, Elon Musk, and Richard Branson. The crazy twists and turns of life and how these incredible people overcome them is truly inspiring. Despite the hundreds of life-accounts I must now have read, there is a familiar omission among the majority of them. Whilst there are often whole chapters dedicated to the successes, there is rarely more than a couple of pages dedicated to the intense grind that takes place behind the scenes of every one of these achievements. World-class athletes have been known to train up to six hours a day to master their craft, racking up tens of thousands of hours of intense exercise that would leave most unable to walk. The lack of communication regarding the extreme commitments success ultimately requires seems strange considering the moment of success itself is usually a short-lived event. Whilst a race can be over in a matter of minutes, the legwork and training can take a lifetime.

It doesn't help that we often tend to compare the everyday moments of our lives to the best moments of others. Social media constantly bombards us with the apparent success of celebrities and entrepreneurs who are often seen driving expensive cars and flashing their expensive houses. We believe their lives are 100 percent better than ours, 100 percent of the time. Instagram and Twitter have brought this phenomenon to our peers too, whether it be envy of friends on vacation whilst you are stuck in your office cubicle or images of other's new cars whilst you're stuck riding the bus. People only tend to show the best bits of their lives, yet we tend to compare these moments to the average parts of ours. Rarely do we get to see or appreciate the years of sacrifice and effort that went into these achievements or personal problems that may be out of sight behind these facades. People tend to show only what they want others to see.

There is little glamour involved in this behind the scenes work, so it is rarely shown. There is rarely any mention of the constant 4 a.m. starts that doctors and athletes commit to for much of their lives without fail. Nor is there much insight highlighting the mental torture from the hundreds of failures and rejections they face. These moments do not inspire us or instill positive emotion, and thus they don't sell. But the hard work hidden behind the scenes constitutes 99 percent of any given achievement. When I look at a gold medal Olympian, I respect that person's ability to relentlessly commit to their craft more than the achievement of the gold medal itself. This is where I believe most self-help books fail. Have you ever read a book and been inspired about the new tools you have learned, only to be back to square one a few months later with no significant change? What is extremely difficult to instill through words is the time and consistency that needs to be dedicated to achieving these goals.

You can read every self-help book under the sun or have a high-level degree from a top-tier university, and still never achieve anything near what you could be capable of. You may have the knowledge to rise to the top of your craft, but knowledge alone provides little tangible benefit. What is also needed is action. I believe action to be more important than knowledge alone. You may know exactly how to start a successful business from start to finish, but if you never take action it is certain you will never build a business. On the other hand, someone who has zero knowledge, but takes action, at least stands a statistical chance, no matter how small, of succeeding due to sheer luck alone. Like how the infinite monkey theorem states that a monkey hitting keys at random on a keyboard for an infinite amount of time will eventually type the complete works of William Shakespeare. The best chances of success stem from the combination of both. With action, you at least stand a small chance. With no action, however, there is no chance at all.

Unfortunately, there is no shortcut or substitution for action. One hour of practice must take one hour of practice. Consistent action requires effort, planning, and experience to successfully progress towards your goals every day. Yet as well-intentioned as our goals may be, and no matter how thoroughly our plans and tasks are set, many goals still fail through lack of action or giving up. I call this point the grind, and this is the largest point of failure in preventing the completion of long-term goals.

No matter what the goal, and how passionate your motivation towards it is, sooner or later you will arrive at a point at which it is no longer fun. Here it turns into a grind. Contrary to common belief, the grind is not a sign that you do not have the willpower or desire to carry out your goal, or a reflection of your character or mental strength, rather it is an inevitable moment originating in the primal chimp whose sole function is to reduce discomfort. Remember we are not in control of our chimp, and therefore cannot be judged by it. It is not a reflection of our character; we can only be judged for our physical actions. The grind, therefore, is not a point where we should get discouraged for not having the mental strength to easily push through, rather it is a point we need to expect and be prepared for when it inevitably arises. The ability to prepare for the grind is what separates professionals from amateurs, and it is vital we do prepare as it is often the first, and most likely, point of failure.

Unfortunately, there is no guaranteed or foolproof method for overcoming the grind. Even with all the motivation and passion in the world, there is simply no stopping the fact that you will be tested by it sooner or later. As we know, willpower is a limited resource insomuch as it cannot be relied upon consistently. What we can do, however, is prepare ourselves as best we can for when it does rear its ugly head.

The systematic techniques outlined in this book, such as the habit table and goal setting document, are vital tools to combat overwhelm. Because failure is almost always emotionally driven, i.e. the chimp wants you to procrastinate because he knows what you are about to do is uncomfortable, we have to take as much of the emotion out of these repetitive tasks as possible. Crafting strong habits and effectively setting goals are systematic and proven ways to transfer the burden of the task from the limbic system (the chimp) onto the prefrontal cortex (the human) by converting goals from emotionally to automatically driven. Once tasks become automatic, there is less chance to become overwhelmed, and therefore less chance to involve the emotional chimp at all. Although still unpleasant, an athlete would find it far less draining to train at 5 a.m. than the average person, not necessarily because they are mentally stronger, but because the habit is better ingrained in them. It doesn't make the task at hand any less demanding, waking up at 5 a.m. is still waking up at 5 a.m., but taking emotion out the equation as much as possible makes quitting far less likely.

Most do not appreciate the difference between envisioning a goal and achieving it. In reality, they are chalk and cheese. Whilst one runs on emotion, the other runs on logic and commitment. In theory, they use entirely separate parts of the brain. The visualization of the goal fires up the chimp, who recognizes that success will feel good, sending bursts of dopamine surging around the body. We therefore rush to plan our goals and put in place actionable steps to move towards it. This is an excellent first step as preached in this book and many others. But this dopamine hit is temporary. In a few weeks, days, or even hours, the reality will dawn upon those who were not mentally prepared to accept the longer-term sacrifices.

When visualizing goals, we need to not only visualize the successes, but also the grind that will be required to achieve it. If you only visualize and plan for the highs, then the lows will take you by surprise (the chimp doesn't like surprises). All of us visualize success, whether it be standing on that podium with a gold medal or buying a Ferrari with the profits from your new business, but very rarely do we visualize the effort, failure and rejections all goals almost certainly contain, such as the daily practice or sleepless nights spent worrying about whether you will be able to pay the next bill. The grind, and how you deal with it, ultimately determines to what extent you succeed. When planning your goals, write a list of all the challenges, failures, and monotonous repetitions you could encounter that might tempt you to give up and how you propose to overcome them. Remember, you cannot avoid the grind, you can only mitigate it as best you can. By having a plan, and entering the challenge already prepared for it, you avoid a lot of the emotional shock that results when the grind first hits. As Baruch Spinoza once quoted: "Emotion, which is suffering, ceases to be suffering as soon as we form a clear and precise picture of it". Better the devil you know than the devil you don't.

When planning for your goals, you have to ultimately weigh up both the highs and the lows to determine whether you are prepared to endure the grind. If you truly want to achieve your goal, the highs should outweigh the lows. If your goal is not something you desire, but rather something which would just be quite nice, the balance may be tilted in the grind's direction and failure is more likely. Perhaps here you can determine that you have other goals that balance the scales more towards the highs. Even if the pain and effort are worth enduring, you are still more likely to fail if you do not adequately prepare for the grind. When planning for your goals, therefore, list out exactly what sacrifices you expect will be needed and how you plan to deal with them. If the challenges are significant, but success from your goals outweighs them, then extensive use of goal planning and habit-building will be necessary. Once you are versed with these techniques, however, and you gather the confidence of successfully overcoming the grind and seeing through your goals, you will have developed an incredibly powerful system for committing to your goals through to completion.

Task:

Take any of your goals. Hopefully, you heeded the advice from the chapter "How to Effectively Set Goals" and defined the what, when and whys of your goal to the true emotional driver. This emotional driver is the high point of your goal, however. To stand the best chance of overcoming the grind, you also need to visualize the low points.

List out all the moments you can think of that might stop you from taking action. Perhaps it is the constant early wake-ups, or the hour of piano practice you need to dedicate every night when you get home from work and all you want to do is collapse on the sofa. You need to visualize yourself facing these grinds to see if you are prepared to endure them. If the visualization of the grind instills more dread than the visualization of your goals instills joy, then your goal is unbalanced and it is therefore likely the grind will engulf you.

2. Learning and Self-improvement

2.1 Create an Insatiable Appetite to Learn

Most would associate learning primarily with periods in school, college, or university, where we obtain the knowledge needed to start a career and pay our way through life. Once we start working, any further learning is usually narrowed towards only that which is needed to perform our jobs. Whilst this has been the basis of the educational systems for decades, learning doesn't, and shouldn't, have to end there. We continue to grow as long as we seek to learn. Those who create an appetite for learning open themselves to more opportunities, in turn creating a richer and more fulfilling life.

Self-motivated learning is what separates a CEO, entrepreneur, or Nobel Laureate from the rest of society. It would be fair to say that most, if not all, successful people have a natural propensity for self-learning, whether they realize it or not. These people tend to be extremely curious by nature. Even celebrities of questionable talent have done their homework on what their version of success looks like. Learning goes far beyond what is taught in schools and read in books. It can be as simple as actively listening to someone who has something of value to share.

Learning is a very broad term and encompasses much. Learning occurs every day whether actively sought or not. It can be large scale, such as taking a company public through an IPO, or simply learning how to operate a new toaster. Both use the same cognitive process and both are equally as important. About a third of human attributes are innate in our DNA, such as skin tone, hair color, sleep patterns, and mood, while the other two-thirds are acquired through learning and experience. This is good news as it means only a third of our attributes are set in stone, implying we can mold the remaining two thirds into whatever we want to be.

Warren Buffet, the world's most successful investor, and current world's fourth-richest man, states that "the best investment one can make, is an investment in oneself... The more you learn the more you'll earn". Mr. Buffet has claimed he spends up to 80 percent of his day reading, starting every morning by scanning an assortment of local and national news articles. The same is true for Bill Gates, Donald Trump, Mark Zuckerberg, and almost every business owner. What links successful people from varying cultures, industries and backgrounds is their appetite for learning.

Learning is no less important for those who are already far into their career. Learning is an essential part of personal and professional development to avoid job stagnation. If you feel like you have reached a stagnant point in your life or career, ask yourself if you have been investing in yourself by learning new skills and trades to progress. Learners are earners, whether that be by accumulating promotions and better jobs or by identifying side businesses such as property development or rentals. Even if you deem yourself already successful, ask yourself when was the last time you actively sought to learn something new or improve your capabilities. Those who learn more identify more opportunities and are better prepared to take them when they arise.

People who seek adult learning opportunities are more socially connected, more involved in their communities, and more likely to be politically active. People in learning environments also have wider and more diverse social circles, creating a network of contacts who provide greater opportunities. Continual learning contributes to higher levels of resilience and self-efficacy in completing a task or tackling a challenge. A construction manager, for example, who is aware of current political and economic events may be better placed to evaluate current property values, identifying higher profit opportunities for both himself and his company.

The modern information age provides almost limitless ways to improve knowledge. Books are one of the staples of learning, with easy access to almost any topic imaginable just a finger click away. Fortunately for you reading this book right now, you are part of this elite actively seeking to grow. Congratulations. More than a quarter of American adults, however, admit to not having read even part of a book within the past year, according to statistics by the Pew Research Center. Experts agree that you can launch yourself into the top 10 percent of people in your field by reading just four books on the topic. Books are relatively cheap considering the sheer value of the content they contain. This book you are reading now, for example, contains a whole lifetime of personal lessons and opportunities for the price of a few cups of coffee. To miss out on such accessible information is truly a shame. To help get you started on this journey, I have included a free eBook of my 10 most recommended books which have influenced me significantly on my decades-long quest for self-improvement. Without having incorporated these books into my life, I certainly wouldn't be writing this one. If you were to follow even 50 percent of the advice and techniques outlined in these books, your competency and quality of life would increase significantly https://jason-strong. ck.page. If you were to read and take action on every book in this list, you would distinguish yourself from 90 percent of your peers.

For learning to be truly successful, however, it needs to be engaging. Many make the mistake of trying to read topics that simply don't interest them. What motivates one person might not motivate another. Find what interests you and pursue it like the quality of your life depends on it. To some extent, it does. Don't read through Shakespeare's dozens of books just because they are in some online list of "30 Books Everyone Should Read At Least Once in Their Lives". Read about business management, science fiction, animals, whatever piques your interest. Reading also provides additional passive benefits that are not immediately recognized. A surprising improvement I found when first starting to read greater quantities and breadth of information was a significant boost in vocabulary and greater confidence with public speaking and writing, traits which are worth their weight in gold in all walks of life.

Reading is not the only means of reading by a longshot, however. The modern wonders of the internet provide many forms of information gathering. Audiobooks are an increasingly common form of learning and can be listened to whilst in the gym or commuting to work. Listening for just an hour a day will allow you to complete a typically sized book in a week. Podcasts are a less formal audio format, with many topics including finance, sports, and news available daily or weekly. Podcasts are an excellent way to accumulate a broad range of knowledge and the informal conversational styles do not require as much concentration so can be played whilst doing other activities, such as housework or whilst at work.

Instead of binge-watching television, try introducing YouTube videos on new topics. YouTube is a mammoth source of information, with over 5 billion videos watched every day, and 300 new videos uploaded every minute. Subscribe to new and interesting channels to discover whole swaths of information and topics you probably never knew existed. If it wasn't for YouTube, I would never even have contemplated tinkering with classic cars. Now I have four!

Online courses are now more popular than ever as people turn towards the plethora of experts available across the internet. Online courses can be informal, such as through user-generated courses on websites such as Udemy, or more formal such as online degrees created by an increasing number of universities. If your career feels like it is stagnating, consider taking some validated online courses to boost both your skillset and your CV. Those who demonstrate that they actively seek self-improvement will prove to any employer that they have a passion for continuous improvement - a very desirable trait employers seek in potential leaders.

Active learning, such as the methods outlined above, is not the only source of education available. Passive learning, such as experiences, conversations, and observations, can often be the most effective way to obtain information not accessible through written material. I truly believe there is something you can learn from every single person on this planet, no matter their status. Conversing, listening, and asking lots of questions is the most engaging way to learn. Genuine curiosity is a trait that can pay for itself a million times over. Ask as many questions as possible from people who have the knowledge to offer. An estimated 10 percent of what we see; 30 to 40 percent of what we see and hear; and 90 percent of what we see, hear, and do is retained by the brain. The more engaging the form of knowledge, the more likely we are to digest it.

The ethos behind this chapter is to develop an insatiable appetite to learn. Think of every experience, whether it be reading a book or meeting a new contact, as an opportunity to better yourself. How successful we become therefore depends on how many of these enriching experiences we can gather. Pursue any interest you have to the maximum degree and always seek creative ways to boost your skillset. Also remember that active learning, such as reading or online courses, covers only a small proportion of available knowledge; the rest lies in viewing others as vast vats of knowledge. Always ask questions about anything you feel may be of benefit to you. Without the mentality of continuous improvement, you risk standing still, and in this day and age, those who stand still fall behind.

Task:

Briefly overview your daily routines and figure out roughly how much time you dedicate to learning or experiencing something new. How much time every day do you spend improving your skillset? Do you feel some stagnancy in your life? Aim to spend at least an hour every day dedicated to learning about something you are interested in, or improving your skillset, whether that be through reading, audiobooks, talking to new people, or joining a new club. You will find days much more gratifying when you feel yourself moving forward.

2.2 Broaden your Reading Material

Most people will readily admit that they should read more. Modern forms of entertainment, such as television, browsing the internet and video gaming seem to have displaced more traditional forms of entertainment, such as reading, especially among younger generations. On average, Americans aged between 20 and 34 spend a mere 16 minutes a day reading. This is truly unfortunate, as reading can be one of the enriching and engaging ways to pass time. The benefits of reading also extend far beyond the content of the book itself.

Joseph Addison, a famous English essayist, poet, and playwright, once quipped that "Reading is to the mind what exercise is to the body". Mental stimulation is incredibly important for the continual long-term health of the brain, ensuring the vast and complex series of neural networks continue to fire at their peak. Without mental stimulation, the brain acts like muscles without exercise - atrophying with little use.

The act of reading, although seemingly effortless, actually requires a delicate, precise, and extremely complex series of neural connections as each part of the brain responsible for different tasks, including visual and auditory processes, phonemic awareness, fluency, and comprehension, all coordinate in a real-time collaborative effort. It can be compared to a symphony orchestra, with various parts of the brain all working together, like sections of instruments, to maximize our ability to decode the written text in front of us. Brain scans have shown that the same neurological regions of the brain which are stimulated by reading are the same regions stimulated by physically experiencing it. According to the ongoing research at Haskins Laboratories, reading, unlike watching or listening to the media, gives the brain time to stop, think, imagine, and process the information in front of us.

Reading is an excellent activity for stimulating the mind and helps keep the brain healthy, while also slowing late-life cognitive decline. A study carried out by researchers from Yale University in the journal 'Social Science and Medicine' found that those who read for up to 3.5 hours a week were 17 percent less likely to die during the study's 12-year research period than those who read no books. Those who read for more than 3.5 hours a week were 23 percent less likely to die. Researcher Becca Levy said: "Older individuals, regardless of gender, health, wealth or education, showed the survival advantage of reading books." She suggested people swap watching TV for reading to help improve life expectancy. She said: "Individuals over the age of 65 spend an average of 4.4 hours per day watching television. Yet old age is the point where ensuring the mind remains stimulated and responsive is more critical than at any other point. Efforts to redirect leisure time into reading books could prove to be beneficial."

Aside from the mental and physical benefits, reading is highly underappreciated as a career booster. Fluent reading (the ability to read quickly whilst retaining a high proportion of information) is a vital skill for top-tier careers which require the ability to pick out vital snippets of information quickly and with great accuracy. Highly compensated careers, such as law, construction, finance, and medicine, all involve complex contracts filled with highly technical clauses which are often written by others to purposely obscure information and potential issues in order to gain an advantage, usually financial. Companies, therefore, pay handsomely for those employees whose reading comprehension allows for the identification of minor and potentially costly details.

Although all important, some forms of reading provide different advantages over others. Nonfiction is important for gathering knowledge and increasing the ability to comprehend technical details. Daily reading on current affairs and global issues provides benefits far beyond just general knowledge; they are excellent social tools, enabling you to participate more meaningfully in social situations where conversations become deeper and cover a wider scope. I have a weekly subscription to the economist magazine which provides 90 percent of my knowledge of what's going on in the world. Other sources include apps and websites such as BBC News and even social media accounts such as Twitter. Find a few reputable online news outlets or apps and make it a daily habit to read them.

Fiction, however, is an underrated tool that has been shown to stimulate greater mental activity than nonfiction, providing additional benefits for the brain such as improved neural connectivity, analytical skills, memory, and vocabulary. Psychologists David

Comer Kidd and Emanuele Castano, at the New School for Social Research in New York, conducted five studies where they evaluated the effects of particular types of reading (genre fiction, literary fiction, nonfiction, and nothing) by testing the groups before and after reading their respective category to determine which provided the greatest improvements. It was found that those who read fiction, and literary fiction in particular, scored the greatest. This genre of fiction prompts the reader to imagine the characters' introspective dialogues. This psychological awareness carries over into the real world, which is full of complicated individuals whose inner lives are usually difficult to fathom. Although literary fiction tends to be more realistic than genre fiction, the characters disrupt reader expectations, undermining prejudices, and stereotypes. They support and teach us values about social behavior, such as the importance of understanding those who are different from ourselves. The value from literary fiction is especially important for children who are still molding their perceptions.

I don't believe there to be good and bad readers, just practiced and unpracticed. Reading is a skill like any other and to reap the benefits one must dedicate time to improve it. Even just a few months of consistent reading will notably improve your ability to read faster while retaining more information, avoiding the need to read passages multiple times for the information to sink in. After a year of avid reading, you should notice your ability to comprehend and retain complex information significantly expand. These skills also help to improve spoken communication.

Anyone can simply read words from a page but to really grasp the meaning behind them, and retain as much of the content as possible, requires training the various parts of your brain to interpret, analyze and retain the information. Start slow; read both fiction and nonfiction on any topic you like as long as it is interesting and engaging. Just because you've been told Charles Dickens is a must-read it doesn't mean it will provide any value to you. Remember, the greatest benefits from reading derives from mental stimulation; if your brain isn't stimulated you will receive little value from it. Just 15 minutes a day will see you complete a book in around 15 days, or 24 books a year. You will be surprised how much value 24 books a year will provide.

Task:

This is simple, read! Dedicate a 15-minute time slot in your schedule to reading anything of interest. Increase this time as you adjust to your daily reading habit. Expand into a broader range of both fiction and nonfiction. But above all ensure whatever you are reading interests you; don't waste time reading books that won't provide any mental stimulation. Also, allocate a few minutes to read the top current affairs headlines daily.

2.3 Realize your Sense of Purpose

Purpose is to life what gas is to a car. You could be the equivalent of a highly tuned race car with all the talent and potential in the world. But with no gas, no motivation, and no sense of purpose, you won't be going anywhere fast.

Finding your purpose may sound like the title of yet another cliché self-help topic, but there is a scientific rationale behind the concept. Numerous journals have found that a sense of purpose appears to have evolved in humans in order to strengthen the survival rates of the species. Those driven by a sense of purpose achieve greater things, such as how Alexander Fleming's relentless passion for the biological sciences led to the discovery of penicillin, which greatly improved survival rates from previously fatal infections. The "sense of purpose" inherent in mankind is simply the brain's primal urge, developed through years of evolution, for chemical gratification (such as dopamine) to encourage us to contribute to the continual survival of the human species, whether this be through simple procreation, or the development of bigger things, such as penicillin.

The reason we feel distressed and depressed when we feel we have no sense of purpose is because our bodies are telling us to change. Similar to how the brain creates feelings of hunger to make us eat, it also creates feelings of unpleasantness (depression and loneliness) by altering levels of neurotransmitters such as norepinephrine, serotonin, and dopamine in the brain. This is a fundamental yet complex biological mechanism that chemically encourages us to change in order to increase the survival rate of the species.

Having a sense of purpose in life is also associated with a lower risk of death, according to a study published in 2019 by the JAMA Network Open. The research, which sampled almost 7,000 people, consisted of a psychological well-being evaluation - a seven-item questionnaire that assessed purpose in life. The study indicated that: "A stronger purpose in life was associated with decreased mortality and that purposeful living may provide health benefits". Although the study is only correlational and not scientific proof, it does reaffirm the notion that a sense of purpose is inherently important to our wellbeing and health. Without it, the body will purposely create feelings of unease for fear we are not contributing to the future prosperity of the human race.

The results from having a burning sense of purpose are clear to see. Steve Jobs was often considered one of the most motivated and driven entrepreneurs of all time, creating what would become the world's first private-sector publicly traded company with a market value of $1 trillion: Apple. Many believe it was his constant need for perfection that drove him to achieve this monumental feat, but his biggest motivation was a desire to leave something behind that changed the way humans engage with technology forever. He wanted to leave a legacy that would change the world for the better. Steve Jobs was not the most talented or intelligent of people, in fact, he was known for his stunning lack of apathy and social skills which led to him being exiled from his own company. But he remained undeterred in his vision and soon found a way back into the company which has since prospered to the giant it has become today even after his death.

Arnold Schwarzenegger was also exceptionally driven to achieve his purpose of becoming the best bodybuilder in the world. Even as a young man in the Austrian army, he woke early every morning to complete thousands of pushups, pull-ups, and anything else he could do with the little equipment and food a bodybuilder typically requires. Everything else was secondary, even his dad passing a few days before a competition would not deter him from missing even one training session. Nothing else mattered, he was only concerned with crafting his body into the best in the world. Both Steve Jobs' and Arnold Schwarzenegger's incredible drives go to show how powerful this primal urge for a sense of purpose truly is.

One must be careful when evaluating their own sense of purpose, however. There is no single purpose we are born to do. Claiming to be "born" to do something is nonsense. Purpose is not some grandiose do or die moment. The only thing required by your purpose is that it quenches the biological mechanism to feel like we are contributing to the prosperity of the species. It needs to involve a sense of achievement, progress, and completion. So when people soul-search and ask, "What should I do with my life?" or "What is my life purpose?" what they actually should ask is: "What can I do with my time that is important and rewards me with a sense of achievement, progress and a point of completion?"

Man's meaning differs from person to person and from day to day. Your purpose is highly individualistic and specific to you and will most likely change with your life experiences and knowledge. You cannot ask a chest master what the best move in the world is for he will tell you this is dependent on many factors such as your opponent, how far into the game you are, or what moves you have previously played. The same is true of our purpose. We must not, therefore, search for some abstract meaning of life, but rather a task that is as unique as your ability to implement it.

Both Steve Jobs and Arnold Schwarzenegger clearly displayed talent and ability. Yet Steve Jobs would not have managed to claw his company back after it was taken away without the fire of purpose motivating him to extreme actions. Motivation, stemming from a clear sense of purpose, separates the successful from the ordinary. I have been on the losing side of this equation many times. I was passed over for a big promotion fairly early on in my career for someone who didn't display as much potential as me; he didn't have a degree and had less experience. On paper, I was clearly superior. But he did have one massive advantage over me; he was extremely motivated. He loved what he did and put in the extra hours and showed more enthusiasm than I ever did, which doesn't go unnoticed. Less intelligent than me or not, he achieved better results because he was far more motivated in search of his purpose, which was clearly him wanting to climb the career ladder as quickly as possible. In hindsight, I'm embarrassed to admit I struggled to understand why I got passed over, but it was a valuable lesson learned relatively early that changed my perspective on how important finding a purpose is in life.

Losing one's way in life, and searching for a sense of motivation and purpose, is a sensation most are likely to encounter at some point. You may have had these very same thoughts yourself. From my experience there are two points in life when the majority of people are likely to begin questioning their sense of purpose; young adults entering the job force for the first time and older generations retiring from it.

I was hit particularly hard by the first of these. Transitioning out of the student life and into the labor market was a terribly confusing time for me. Although the two periods of my life, studying and working, were similar in structure - working from 7 a.m. to 5 p.m. every weekday - I was never concerned with the everyday grind that these monotonous patterns created whilst studying. My five-year university course was a means to an end; a temporary sacrifice to secure a life of comfort and relative wealth. That was my motivating goal and sense of purpose and five years was a short enough period for me to be able to see the light at the end of the tunnel. Although the fatigue of studying set in by the fifth year, as the lack of money and diet consisting primarily of beans and noodles wore thin, the end was in sight and the purpose of creating a life of relative wealth and comfort was within arm's reach.

I couldn't wait to finish university and start releasing my dream of entering the workplace. Just a few months into my first job, however, saw me start to question my original sense of purpose. Every early wake up was immediately followed by "why do I need to get out of bed? What's the point of going to work?" Without the motivation of graduating, I had nothing to look forward to and progress towards. There was no chemical gratification that my primal urges demanded. The realization for many young adults that life will consist of the same routine for the next 40 or 50 years can cause significant grief and often lead to depression. This depression is the body's way of telling you that you have no clear purpose.

A similar phenomenon can be found when it comes to retirement. Having dedicated most of their life to building a career, the sudden lack of direction and purpose which work previously provided can be overwhelming for many retirees. There have been multiple academic studies noting an increase in strokes and heart diseases immediately after retirement. According to a study by the London-based Institute of Economic Affairs, the likelihood that someone will suffer from clinical depression increases by about 40 percent after retiring. The lack of purpose can be majorly overwhelming, and the stress can cause health issues.

No matter the age there are steps that can be taken to help discover or develop a motivating purpose. Many find it in family, such as having children or caring for aging relatives. The motivation to provide and give their children every possible advantage to succeed in life is a very strong evolutionary instinct that can provide a significant sense of purpose for some. Others want to cure cancer or change the world for the better. A new hobby or blog can also fill this void. No motivating passion or purpose is too big or small, the only error is in not finding a purpose at all. Remember, your body doesn't know (or care) what your purpose is, it is only concerned with quenching the primal urges to feel a sense of direction for the purpose of continuing the health of the species. Find your purpose in whatever fills this void.

Avoid looking for purposes which you feel must be validated by other people. Becoming wealthy or inventing the next printing press, whilst certainly fulfilling achievements, may not define success for you. Just because society values doctors more highly than musicians does not mean a sense of purpose cannot be found through music. Throughout my teens and twenties, I strength trained daily, a sacred ritual I kept up for decades. Unfortunately, I was never gifted with perfect genes like Arnold Schwarzenegger, and never reached a stage where I could perform professionally, but the progress I saw every year in both my physique and strength was a huge sense of purpose that encapsulated me. I never made any money, nor received any kind of recognition, it was just something where success was personally defined by me through progress. No matter the ups and downs in my life, the one thing that kept me going throughout the day was knowing that I was progressing in my biggest passion.

There is no real guide or method to actively find a sense of purpose. Each individual is different and will have a definition of success that is unique to them. I can only offer two real pieces of advice: first, always pursue anything that interests you. After years of imagining myself being able to play the piano, I finally drew the motivation to learn it, something I had always assumed I was too old and too busy to do. It really did give me a boost of motivation, having a daily goal of improving my piano skills. So, whatever your interest, find a way to pursue and expand upon it.

For many, this will mean seeking new experiences to find out what your passions and motivations may be. Read, join clubs, always say yes to new experiences and create an insatiable appetite to learn new things. New interests will arise out of new experiences that may never have surfaced had we not actively sought them.

The second, and perhaps most profound tip, is to find and cherish your true identity. By this I mean find out who you really are and what you care about. Only those who truly know themselves, their strengths, weaknesses, and motivations, can seek a life that aligns with it. Always keep your identity at the forefront of your mind whatever you do. It will always be more difficult to find something to pursue in life when we haven't thoroughly discovered what motivates us. The next chapter outlines exactly what is meant by our identity and how we can set about discovering it.

Task:

Take a look at your daily routine. What activities during your day are geared directly toward your purposes or goals? Are you even aware of your purpose?

If you have a feeling of emptiness in your life similar to that described above, where your career or family life feels stagnant, you may well be suffering from a lack of purpose, the body's way of telling you that you are not contributing to the continued prosperity of yourself or the species. Go out, explore the world, and find your identity to develop this sense of purpose.

To narrow this down, avoid asking generic questions such as "What should I do with my life?" or "What is my life purpose?". What you should actually be asking is "What can I do with my time that is important to me and rewards me with a sense of achievement, progress, and a point of completion?". No purpose, big or small, is less valuable than another.

2.4 Find your Identity

This tip is so important I had to devote a separate chapter to it. Simply put, we can define identity as the naturally occurring qualities that make us who we are as individuals. Some have a greater propensity for adrenaline-seeking whilst others are more entertained by opera. There is no identity greater than another, the variation is what makes humanity so interesting.

Tony Robbins, American author, public speaker, life coach, and philanthropist, calls identity the most powerful force in human nature. Strong knowledge of our identity should drive our decisions in a direction that pushes us toward our goals. When our self-identity is weak, we act without thinking how it aligns with our identity, resulting in questionable decisions we later come to regret.

Finding your identity goes much further than simple questions such as "who am I?" or "what do I want in life?". Finding your identity cannot be answered by asking simple questions, it must be discovered through your life experiences, where you experience your highest highs and your lowest lows. You must experience these highs and lows, and see how you respond to them, to really understand your character. You have to engage these externalities in order to prove to yourself how tough you are mentally and what really motivates you in life. It is a gradual process that takes effort and time and we need to work at finding it relentlessly until we are confident in ourselves.

I believe a large portion of humanity goes through life without fully realizing their maximum potential. Identity is not an analog trait, but rather a scale of how strongly we understand, believe, and live by our values. Trying to live in a way that's inconsistent with our true nature will create a life of frustration, stress, and disappointment. We must learn to embrace our deepest needs, desires, strengths, fears, values, and beliefs in order to create harmony and tap into our tremendous potential. Anyone, such as myself, who went through a large portion of their life with a nice job, nice house, fancy car, and wonderful family, yet still felt like something was missing, are most likely missing the part of life that fuels their identity. The problem for these people, however, is that they are so comfortable in their lives that they are rarely able to leave their comfort zone to find it.

Terrifying past life experiences and trauma, whilst certainly not recommended, are often key foundations of one's identity. Man's Search for Meaning, the 1946 bestselling memoirs of Viktor Frankl, chronicles Viktor's experiences as a prisoner in Nazi concentration camps during World War II and describes how he coped in an environment where your chance of dying each day was greater than surviving. Viktor stated how he had to identify a purpose in his life to feel positive about, and then immersively visualizing that outcome. Many of today's most successful people, including rappers 50 Cent and Eminem, emerged out of traumatic childhoods involving drugs, domestic abuse, and death. The fact is, however, these experiences toughen your mental attitude and enable you to find mental courage in times of despair.

I don't like dramatics, but you will never, ever achieve anywhere near what you are capable of without discovering your identity. It is impossible. There are too many forces at play that try to hinder you. The "comfort zone" is what holds most of us back, which niggles away at you every time you try to leave it. Most can't break through these mental barriers because they have no reason to; they have no purpose or identity to pull them through. I found myself in this position for much of my life.

How can you become the fastest 100m sprinter without identifying that you are one of the best athletes in the world? Or as David Goggins, a retired Navy SEAL turned ultramarathon runner puts it, how can you run a 130-mile ultra-marathon through Death Valley at the peak of summer unless you know you are "the toughest son of a bitch on the planet"? How can you win Mr. Olympia, the height of bodybuilding perfection, seven times without knowing you are the best bodybuilder in the world? You can't, period.

To achieve our full potential, and unlock all the rewards associated with it, we need the mental strength to push through our comfort zones and the intense short-term pain. Knowing our identity, and why exactly we are doing what we are doing, whether it be running a marathon or moving your family across the state for a new promotion, will help you release that inner strength.

Identity is one of the fundamental foundations of mental toughness. It strengthens your character. That is, when we know who we are, have confidence in ourselves, and are able to identify our strengths, we emerge as stronger individuals. It gives you that extra oomph to keep fighting when most would succumb to the pain. It is the force that compels you to keep running when you hit "the wall". Like compound interest, these experiences of you winning over your mind compound into greater senses of accomplishment, which you can draw upon when you next find yourself mentally challenged, helping you achieve even greater feats and accomplishments. It is an iterative process of self-improvement which allows you to continually achieve greater things.

For some people, their identity is identified early on in life. It is a life mission that seems inherent in childhood. For Arnold Schwarzenegger, it was to become the best bodybuilder on the planet. For Warren Buffet it was to become the richest man on Earth. For most others, however, finding this identity, and therefore sense of purpose, feels like finding a needle in a haystack. Unless you know exactly where to look.

The simple fact is, to find your identity you have to find your lowest and most insecure moments. There is no way around it. You will never fully know who you are or what you›re about if you never test your mental toughness. How can you find yourself if you never look? People who have gone through hard times have found their lows and the fact they survived through them hardens them and strengthens their minds. David Goggins, author of the bestselling title "Can't Hurt Me" refers to this as callusing the mind. Similar to how your hands build callouses every time you lift heavy weights in a bid to protect your skin next time you lift, traumatic events can callous your mind in a similar manner. If you have gone through life cushioned, with little trouble and always being average at everything, you will have very little mental callusing and are therefore much more likely to give up when you are mentally challenged. There is no way you can truly know or believe in your identity if you haven't experienced these callusing moments.

To find it, therefore, you need to experience mentally challenging moments. For those who have had a comfortable life, as I had, you need to actively seek mentally challenging experiences. Sign up for a marathon, take an online course you always wanted to do, or end that relationship you feel has you locked or unable to improve yourself, despite the mental anguish you know it might cause. Leave that dead-end job you know is ruining your sense of worth or happiness. You may be financially burdened for some time, have to move, or start all over again but these are the prices to pay for a better life. Your life won't improve or turn into what you dreamed it will be by itself, life doesn't work like that, nor should it. Get out of your comfort zone and seek challenges, seek fear, and seek a way to overcome them. Make a note of your success every time you overcome these tough challenges and draw upon these successes when you are next challenged. By winning these mental games, we build our library of successful memories which we can call upon when times get tough. Only by testing the extreme ends of your mentality can you create that life you always wanted.

What is my identity? For me, my identity is doing whatever I want to do with my life, being my own boss, and ensuring every minute I spend on this earth is for me and those important to me. This identity came late for me, however. I had a comfortable past and had no real identity until near my 30s. Eventually, the mediocrity became wearing, doing the same thing over and over again. I looked at all these successful people and noted how comfortable they were with failure. They didn't care if they failed, they didn't care what people thought of them. They never gave in to rejection despite being continually denied whatever they were chasing. Why couldn't I be like that? Why did I care so much about what other people thought of me? Why was I so mentally weak? In the end, this became my trauma. I was fed up with being average and not being able to push myself, a thought which started to eat away at me every minute of every day. Eventually, I came to the conclusion of what I have explained; that I hadn't yet developed my identity. Although many successful people have built this through life experiences, I had not. I had to go out and seek it, which meant finding every opportunity to seek fear and bring myself to my weakest and most exposed moments. I signed up for long-distance runs, despite a passionate hate for running, quit my nice job, and moved abroad. Ironically, I never felt more in control than when I gave these things up.

There is nothing more comforting and rewarding in life than truly knowing your identity and what you are capable of. All those years of working for somebody else, sacrificing my time for someone's gain kept me in a mental cage and kept me from developing my identity and achieving success in my life that I always dreamed of. This is one of the reasons I first moved away from England. I had a well-paying job, company car, free accommodation but I still felt trapped. So, I packed it all up and left to get out of my comfort zone. I dread to think where I would be if I hadn't made this decision. No doubt I would have been comfortable, but mentally I would have always had that internal pain. Eventually, you get so sick of the internal pain it starts to become more painful than the pain of actually doing what it is you are dreading. The relief you feel breaking away from your comfort zone eventually outweighs the pain involved in actually doing it.

So, to those who are struggling to find their identity, go out, and first find your mental strength, who you are and what you are made of. Sign up for that marathon, online course, or quit that job you hate. No matter how well you think you know your identity you can always strengthen this bond. Yes, it›s going to be tough. Yes, there will be times when you regret making those decisions, but in order to create that life you always envisioned you have to find your identity, which is born out of discovering your mental strength.

Task:

Try to write and precisely define your identity. Who are you? What gets you out of bed every morning? What mental experiences can you draw upon when things get tough? Write out some of the most painful or traumatic experiences you have overcome, no matter how small or insignificant they may seem.
When was the last time you truly pushed through your comfort zone and achieved something great? More importantly, what can you do from now on to put you through these moments and start building your mental strength and endurance. Physical activity is a great way to build these connections. Sign up for something that you know will test you beyond your comfort zone. Every mental success when overcoming tough times will strengthen your identity, and therefore your capabilities.

2.5 Travel

"The world is a book, and those who do not travel read only one page"- Saint Augustine. There is no amount of reading that can encapsulate the enlightenment from traveling. The world is full of wonders that are beyond even the most creative of minds and must be experienced in person to be believed. In an age of fast and relatively inexpensive flights, one can travel almost anywhere in the world within 18 hours. There are a myriad of benefits to traveling beyond wealthy students "finding themselves" during gap years.

For a start, there is simply no better way to learn about the world than to be part of it first-hand. You can read to your heart's content but the emotion involved, whether it be joy or fear, in physical experiences is by far the most engaging and fun way to learn. Whether it be a tour of the Alamo in San Antonio or visiting the Abba museum in Stockholm, I have emerged from each travel destination more knowledgeable than when I entered.

By far the most enriching traveling experiences, however, occur when you learn more about yourself. As mentioned in the previous chapter, seeking and engaging with all manner of experiences and opportunities is one of the best ways to discover your identity. Travelling is an excellent way to actively seek experiences and it forces you out of your comfort zone where your identity is tested. When I first traveled alone to Canada, I was a completely different person to when I flew back just five years later. I grew older, wiser, and more aware of my identity; I knew my fundamental character, flaws, and all, and understood what is important and what motivates me.

My first accomplishment was in finding a job. It took a few anxiety-inducing weeks of living on rapidly diminishing savings for me to find my first job in construction. During this time, I had to find a place to live, obtain a social insurance number, get my driver's license and call around begging and searching for work. I was so overwhelmed that those first four weeks felt like years. But after two months of scraping by, I looked back at my progress in astonishment, not just with what I had achieved, but how I had conducted myself. I had a very good job which I was settling into nicely, I had overcome the many hurdles needed to obtain my social insurance number and was finally able to travel around (despite the pain and embarrassment of failing my driver's license test the first time around). But more importantly, I had shown determination and an ability to stay calm, keep my head down and persevere through the overwhelm. For someone who always thought of themselves as shy and timid, I sure knew how to get things done when I needed to. This feat was added to my mental library of accomplishments, which I drew upon many times when I questioned my identity and needed a confidence boost.

My self-discovery continued from here. As time passed and experiences grew, I became noticeably more confident in solving problems and overcoming obstacles, benefitting me greatly in both my personal and professional life. My perception of difficulty had shifted greatly enabling me to tackle greater problems with less stress. Instead of facing a state of overwhelm when confronted with a new problem, I drew upon my previous conquests to keep calm and collected. Problems turned more into simple challenges. When I got my first job, I had to move shortly afterward to reduce my commute. Whereas finding an apartment the first-time around was one of the most anxiety-inducing activities of my life, the second time around was far easier.

Anyone who has traveled for a significant period of time will attest to the fact that traveling changes you physiologically. It induces confidence in your general competence and ability to adapt. This is a trait that employers pay handsomely for, from project managers to surgeons and CEOs. The ability to keep calm and act rationally under pressure in rapidly changing environments is what all employers seek in high-level leaders. Traveling, especially when outside of your comfort zone, is about the best practice one can get in obtaining these traits. It doesn't just get you used to going outside your comfort zone, it expands your comfort zone altogether, enabling you to achieve greater things without even having to leave it.

For those who are struggling to find their identity and a sense of purpose as described in the previous two chapters, traveling can be one of the most influential tools in helping you discover it. Having first entered the workforce after graduating from university, I could only withstand five years of the daily grind before I could barely muster the effort to get out of bed. For the five years after moving to Canada, however, this feeling was completely replaced by new emotions of anxiety, fear, joy, and a sense of accomplishment of trying to thrive in a new environment. Although there were times of extreme stress and anxiety, the one emotion I no longer felt was boredom. Those five years were among the five most exciting of my life. I learned I was able to endure the lows with the highs but what I couldn't endure were feelings of boredom and nothingness. I realized a significant part of my purpose was to uncover my identity and find out exactly what motivates me and what my strengths and weaknesses were. A large part of this was simply in never standing still. Even in times where I felt I was progressing backward, such as when passed over for a job by a junior colleague, I still felt I was discovering more about myself which would pay dividends later in life. After five years of living in Canada, I decided to move back to the United Kingdom when feelings of missing family set in. My identity morphed with time and my aging family became an increasingly important component of my identity. At this point, my identity and purpose had shifted, so I had to adapt.

Upon returning back to England there was one social benefit from traveling I noticed immediately. Small talk did not just become easier, it became fun. I found my stories and memories made me more interesting to others and opened lots of avenues for questions. Whereas small talk would normally involve filling awkward voids with meaningless verbiage, others were now doing the hard work for me since they were so intrigued about my stint abroad. It's funny how many people have cousins, friends, or relatives who live in Canada and they always wanted to travel there. Other people pick up on your stories and experience which makes it more natural and engaging to communicate with people.

The most influential part of traveling, however, was the lifelong memories I obtained, which are my most cherished possessions I own today and are still as vivid as the day I experienced them. I can still taste the world's best BBQ from my adventures in Austin, Texas and I can still feel the glorious heat on my skin from surfing in California. I can even remember the first time I was stung by a wasp in the quaint little town of Lubeck, Germany. You can have all the money and fame in the world, but do you think you'll be thinking about these during your last few days on earth? I like to think my last moments will be a mental collage of all the most memorable moments of my life, most of which were accumulated whilst exploring both the world and myself.

I have spoken a lot of traveling the world, but it is important to remember that traveling need not be limited solely to other countries, the expense of which can be beyond many budgets. I define traveling as simply experience gathering in new places outside your immediate comfort zone. Whilst I certainly recommend traveling as much of the world as possible, for those less fortunate in terms of time or money you can travel within your own country. There are always tours, museums, parks, and open areas ready to be explored. Half the benefit of traveling lies in the memories obtained; the location in which this is done hardly matters.

2.6 See Mistakes as Opportunities to Learn

Benjamin Franklin once quipped, "There are only two things certain in life: death and taxes". I would add a third - failure. Failure is a dirty word that is often taken way too seriously. It is viewed with great embarrassment, serving only to dishearten and discourage. Yet failing offers one of the most effective learning tools available to man. In fact, making mistakes is the most fundamental component of the biological learning mechanism. The primary reason humans have emerged the dominant species is through our advanced ability to quickly learn from trial and error. Yet the modern man will go to extraordinary lengths to avoid failure to almost any degree, even at the detriment of self-improvement.

Ironically, failure is the most efficient path to success. A child, for example, is never taught how to walk. It is an ability they pick up naturally by learning from failure. Each trip and fall sends neurons flying around the brain, building increasingly more capable neural networks and continually strengthening the mind-muscle connection. Each failure results in another piece of information for the central nervous system to build upon, inching closer to success one failure at a time.

Failure doesn't discourage a child from learning to walk like it would an adult going through the same process. Despite taking weeks or even months to progress from a cute crawling blob to a daring drunken sailor, they never stop trying. Learning from failure is the most basic human learning trait in existence, yet by the time we reach adulthood we begin to lose this passion for learning and begin to fear it. For many, it eventually stops us from even trying.

Many academic studies have found a strong correlation between a fear of failure and the school education system. School systems are very black and white, usually culminating in passing or failing an exam. Failing exams often have dire consequences; low grades can be the sole criteria for not getting into college or taking a specific course. The stakes are extremely high. To make matters worse, school curriculums do not properly encourage exploration of ideas or encourage us to softly fail. Instead of exploiting our inherent biological learning mechanism, we are taught one way to do things - everything else is considered wrong. Whereas humans can be said to learn from the bottom up (i.e. we start at our most incapable and become increasingly competent the more we fail and learn) schools teach in the opposite manner - from the top down.

I remember learning how to integrate and differentiate equations at school. We were taught the exact process for how to perform it and I mastered it very quickly. It soon became my strongest aspect of mathematics. Yet when an exam question tested how to differentiate outside of the context I learned it in, the fundamental lack of understanding was clear to see. I had learned it through memory as opposed to a fundamental understanding and therefore couldn't solve it because it was not presented in the exact manner in which I had learned it. It can be compared to trying to drive a car just through watching videos online. While you may know the exact technicalities of how to operate a vehicle, it is not until you fail by stalling the car a dozen times that you start to build neural pathways between feet and brain that really teach you how to drive a car. Schools need to teach not by telling students how to drive the car, but by letting them stall a dozen times in a safe and encouraging setting.

As adults, we have the ability to change our perception of failure. We need to see failure not as a value of our self-worth, but as the fundamental component of our wonderful natural learning mechanism. Without failure, we would not be capable of learning nearly as quickly or effectively. This is why the most experienced entrepreneurs know they need to fail hard and fail fast. Failure breaks only those who see it as an absolute loss, as an end in itself. What separates a successful entrepreneur from an unsuccessful one is not a greater level of intelligence (although it certainly helps) but in becoming an expert at failing. When failure inevitably occurs, successful people correlate this in a more positive manner, seeing it as another step closer to their ultimate goal. Extroverts tend to find this more instinctive as they care less of what others think and are more concerned with their own betterment. Introverts, on the other hand, are more likely to be influenced by what others think of them, leading them to become more risk-averse through fear of looking foolish.

The savviest entrepreneurs are those who use their many failures as building blocks to keep rising higher as quickly as possible. That is why they never get tired of trying, no matter how often they fail. Arguably America's greatest inventor, Thomas Edison, had an extraordinarily positive perception of failure that greatly enhanced his ability as an inventor. Where others would have become hopelessly discouraged after failing over a thousand times in an attempt to invent the electric lightbulb, Edison simply viewed each unsuccessful experiment as the elimination of a solution that wouldn't work, thereby moving him one attempt closer to a successful one. We could all take a lesson from Edison. I once read of a miner who struck gold just a few meters beyond where another had just given up after days of back-breaking digging, creating wealth that lasted generations. There are few obstacles in life that cannot eventually be overcome by consistent, intelligent, and positive action. When you next find yourself discouraged after failing, remember Edison's near 1,000 failures before he finally arrived at the solution that changed the world forever.

That being said, failing is only the means of learning, not the end. Failing for the sake of failing, where no lessons are learned, will not result in any form of progress. As Henry Ford said, "The only real mistake is the one from which we learn nothing." This means we have to spend time analyzing the mistake and working out exactly why it occurred and how to avoid making the same mistake on subsequent attempts.

Believe it or not, failing (or rather, learning from failure) is a skill like any other and requires experience and a positive mindset to continually improve. It requires the ability to see the benefits which arise from failing, i.e. the knowledge learned for a more successful attempt next time round. What defines a successful person is not how often they fail, but how fast they can recover and learn from it.

Once you are well versed in the art of learning from failure, your resilience will increase exponentially. Instead of the fear of failure-inducing procrastination and feelings of overwhelm, it will draw you to action. When you inevitably hit your first stumbling block, your momentum will remain unchanged as your mistakes are associated in a positive manner as opposed to a negative one. As Winston Churchill once said, "Success is stumbling from failure to failure with no loss of enthusiasm."

"Fail fast and recover quickly". That oft-cited catchphrase is behind some of the greatest learning experiences I've had in both my business and personal life. The first step in changing your attitude to failure is to first acknowledge it. Next time you make a mistake, make the conscious effort to analyze it. First, understand that it is perfectly natural to feel discouraged and disheartened. Secondly, analyze the failure to identify any lessons learned. Lastly, and this is most often the most difficult part, do not dwell on the mistake after you have identified the lesson learned. This is easier said than done and is almost impossible to eliminate completely, but this is the thought process you need to follow to make you a better learner. With time and experience, your mentality towards failure will turn from destructive to productive and you will have learned one of the most valuable tools in a successful person's arsenal.

Task:

Next time you encounter a failure of some kind, follow the checklist of actions below to turn it from a discouraging negative into a positive:

1.   Acknowledge that you have failed and that this is perfectly acceptable and reasonable. Even it seems like a stupid mistake, we are all human and prone to mistakes. It is inevitable. Understand that many have probably made, and will continue to make, the same mistake.

2.   Remember that you are not defined by the mistake, just on how quickly you act to fix it. That is the only power in our immediate control.

3.   Analyze exactly where you went wrong. Make a list of everything that could have gone better and next to each one, write a solution for how you would avoid this error if you were to do it again.

2.7 Always Think of the Bigger Picture and Never Dwell on Negative Thoughts

Dwelling on the past is like reading the same chapter over and over again while expecting the story to change. We can't change past events, yet we still tend to replay them in our minds on repeat. Holding onto lingering feelings not only prevents us from moving onto bigger and better things but also traps us in a metaphoric box of frustration, prolonging the pain. We all know the key to a productive and successful life is to always keep moving forward whilst leaving past problems behind, yet we still can't help but dwell on trivial and insignificant events.

Some are naturally more prone to lingering thoughts than others. The likes of Steve Jobs and Elon Musk rarely give a second thought to rejection, failure, or embarrassment. They don't care because their goals and passions create a wonderfully productive tunnel vision; no task or event that does not directly progress them one step closer to their goals is even worth thinking about. For the rest of us mere mortals more prone to negative thinking, however, dwelling on past events is an everyday battle. Whether it be a social miscue or failing at work, we all have those moments where we wish the earth would just open up and swallow us whole. My common flashback was during my early teens when I thought trapping my friend in the bathroom would be hilarious. When it turned out to be her elderly grandmother, however, it was not so funny (although my friend found it hysterical). As silly as it seems I still look back in embarrassment and cringe at this memory.

Our chimp will almost always make events like these seem worse than they actually are. To help combat this initial overreaction, seek to place the event in its true context. For example, your first break up can seem like the end of the world when the shock of it first hits you. Once time passes, and a more suitable partner is found, we can look back with the power of hindsight and see that it was no big deal in the grand scheme of life. In fact, it may have been a blessing as it allowed for the meeting of someone more appropriate. Placing events in their true context is a skill that comes with age and experience and is generally more difficult for the younger and less experienced. Having been particularly prone to dwelling on the past myself, I devised a small mental test to help surround an event in its true context. I call it the "three-ones" rule as we ask ourselves three simple questions about the consequences of the mistake in one week, one month, and one year's time.

The first question is, will this event be significant in one week? I find that most negative events we think are a big deal fail to get beyond even this first stage. Let's say you missed numbers in your cost report that means the accounts are now imbalanced and need to be redone. This may be embarrassing if in front of your peers or superiors, but the problem is easily remedied and will not be significant next week when it will most likely be forgotten entirely. Maybe you messed up in a job interview or argued with your partner; whatever the problem it is more often not quickly forgotten. If the answer to this first question of the "three-ones" is no, i.e. the event won't be significant in one week, then in the greater context of life the issue is moot and deserves no more mental capacity dedicated to it. Fail fast, learn your lesson and tell your chimp that it does not matter. Eventually, he will subside and fall in line. If you answered yes to this first question, however, and the event will be significant in a week, move on to question number two.

Question two; will the event be significant in one month. If the answer is no then you have a short-term problem (between 1-4 weeks) that does indeed require some attention and thought to resolve. Remind yourself that we cannot be judged for making mistakes, for we are all human and inevitably make mistakes. We will, however, be judged for how quickly we fix it. Understand that your chimp is responsible for your thoughts of unease and box it as quickly as possible. Only once the chimp has been calmed can you then start to devise a rational and logical plan for overcoming this short-term problem. For example, your accounting mistake now means you have to come in every Saturday, unpaid, for the next few weeks to backtrack and correct all data in time for next month's report. Although understandably frustrating, a few weeks in the context of life is not such a big deal and a short-term effort will remedy the situation. There is an end in sight, it is just a case of dedicating the time needed to get there. Remember questions one and two in this rule are short term and can be fixed with a relatively short time commitment. Most importantly, they will soon become insignificant and most likely forgotten once complete.

If you answered yes to question two, i.e. the problem will still be significant in over one month, move on to the third and final question: will the event be significant in more than one year? If no, then you have a medium-term problem that will certainly require time and effort to rectify. But there will be an end and the speed at which you react and attempt to rectify the problem determines how long this recovery will take. For example, your accounting error means the company now faces financial fines for misrepresenting its accounting statistics, and as such you were fired. You have a dependent family back home that relies solely on your income and you have very little savings. Undoubtedly, the next few months will be very tough, and the event will take a substantial amount of time and effort to recover from. You will have to trawl through hundreds of advertisements in search of a new job. You may even have to take a lower-paying job temporarily just to get some cash flowing. Your family will have to make cutbacks to make ends meet, most likely putting a strain on your relationship. But what is important is to identify the context of the situation within the bigger picture. In a few months, you will most likely be back working with the worst behind you. Each day will see your situation improve. Many become emotionally overwhelmed in the initial moment which only serves to worsen the situation. Negative reactions are understandable and inevitable, but you have the power (and responsibility if you have dependents) to box the chimp and start thinking rationally in order to mitigate the damage. It can be easy to get carried away with these powerful emotions and fall into a hole of self-despair, but by asking yourself the "three-ones" questions, and finding in which category you currently lie, can you then place the issue into the bigger context of life, helping contain the spiral of runaway emotions and ground your thoughts. Once grounded, it will be easier to climb back up to where you last fell. You may even find an opportunity to climb higher than before. Yes, it is a tough position to be in but most bounce back, some stronger than before. Humans are incredibly resilient; how quickly you recover, however, depends on your ability to place your error in its true context and therefore gain control over your emotions.

Those unfortunate enough to have answered yes to all three questions, however, should recognize that they may have a severe problem that will take considerable time and resources to overcome. Poor health is the most common factor here, whether it be you or a family member. I have recently learned of an old friend whose wife, his life and joy, has early-onset dementia. He now has to retire early to spend the remainder of his wife's life taking care of her through this deeply traumatic event. Issues that span a great length of time will be very draining and consume every waking second of your life. The end is vague - who knows how long this situation will occur for- and the end is tragic in itself; death. The best option I can suggest here is to seek professional help. What's worse than going through these traumas at all is going through them alone, as loneliness is the prime breeding ground for runaway negative emotions. Therapists can help you put your problems in perspective which at least helps you to understand and accept them, the first step in dealing with them.

To recap, the "three-ones" should be used to ask yourself three progressive questions whenever you feel overwhelmed by emotion, either by an event in your life beyond your control or by a mistake you made that is embarrassing or damaging. These three questions will help place your problem in its holistic context, determining whether the problem will be significant in one week, one month, or one year. A problem lasting less than a week is the most common where many overreact without realizing how insignificant it is in the true context of life. The problem will be resolved in less than a week so stop wasting any more time dwelling on it and move on. A problem lasting greater than one week but less than a month will require time and effort to rectify, and short-term emotional turmoil may accompany it, but in the greater context of life, a few months requires only short-term sacrifice and the end will be in sight. Knuckle down and get it over with as quickly as possible. A problem lasting greater than one month but less than a year, however, may be fairly significant and affect your quality of life for the foreseeable future. Although great attention and effort will be required to overcome it, the problem is again only temporary. Answering yes to all three questions, however, justifies emotional overwhelm and external help will most likely be needed. Fortunately, this is the least common category.

This line of thinking, often referred to as "big picture" thinking, is an incredibly powerful quality of a good leader. It is a skill that distinguishes the most successful of people and one which employers compensate highly. Like any other skill, it can be practiced with time and experience but requires a certain amount of mindfulness to analyze these events as they happen in their bigger context. The "three-ones" technique helps introduce this mindfulness.

One of the most prominent examples of big picture thinking in modern history is by Sir Winston Churchill, the prime minister of the United Kingdom from 1940 to 1945 when he led Britain to victory in the Second World War. In the delicate few months leading up to the outbreak of war in 1938, Great Britain was debating on whether to agree to appeasement with Adolf Hitler. Hitler, having already invaded Austria and Czechoslovakia with little to no opposition, wanted to sign an appeasement treaty, in effect guaranteeing peace with Great Britain in exchange for control of all areas with greater than 50 percent German occupancy. Neville Chamberlain, then prime minister, was an avid supporter of appeasement along with the majority of the nation, including much of the media and the British public who were still physically and mentally scarred from the horrors of the First World War. Chamberlain signed the Munich Agreement with Hitler, allowing him to take land from Czechoslovakia. The British peoples celebrated, thinking they had avoided another war.

Yet Winston Churchill was not part of that group. Churchill could have ridden on the public support for appeasing and avoided going to war. But he couldn't. It went against every one of his moral fibers because he saw the big picture. In his now infamous 1938 Munich speech, he stated how Chamberlain's treaty was dishonorable and pointless as war was inevitable. He was able to place the problem in the greater context of life and see that this predicament would still be a problem in more than a year even if the treaty was signed. Hitler was a fanatic and his grand vision of a reborn German empire would not end with a signature on a piece of paper but would only die with him. In his speech to the British parliament, who were deciding whether or not to go to war, everyone in that room could visualize the grave consequences of fighting, for most had lived through the bloody slaughter just 22 years before. There was scarcely a family in Britain that had not been touched by sorrow. Was it right – was it fair – to ask the people to go through all that again? And to what end? He knew appeasement would essentially by a white flag raised over Britain. Churchill went on to give his masterpiece of a speech to the nation, stating "If this long island story of ours is to end at last, let it end only when each one of us lies choking in his own blood upon the ground."

Within a year of that decision – to fight and not to negotiate – 30,000 British men, women, and children had been killed, almost all of them at German hands. Weighing up the alternatives – a humiliating peace, or a slaughter of the innocents – it is hard to imagine any modern British politician having the guts to take Churchill's line.

He had the spirited and almost reckless moral courage to see that fighting would be appalling, but that surrender would be even worse. History now reckons he was right. And it is thanks to his big picture thinking, and putting the future of Great Britain ahead of himself, and all those who fought for British freedom, that the Nazi regime was not allowed to continue on its tyrannical path. The moral here is that true success stems from being able to place events in their long-term context, as opposed to getting trapped in short-term emotions. The short-term consequences may be severe, as they were for Britain, but they must be weighed against potential longer-term issues, which may be even worse.

Task:

Have this checklist on hand when you (inevitably) next find yourself dwelling on past events or blunders. By being prepared, you can better fight off the initial overwhelm and recover quicker.

1.   Understand that your chimp is highly reactive right now and is most likely overreacting. Allow it to vent, settle, and then place the event in its greater context of life once the rational human thoughts have returned.

2.   Ask yourself the "three-ones" questions: Will it matter in one week, one month, or one year? Place your issue into one of these bands to better understand what actions need to be taken to mitigate damages. Remember you are only judged for how you react to events and you have a duty to mitigate damages as best you can.

3.   Once you have banded your problem, you now have a more holistic view of your situation. From here you can create a plan and contextualize your problem by figuring out how you are going to solve your problem and how long this might take.

By following this procedure, you will not only overcome your problem much quicker, but you will also reduce the unnecessary amount of negative thinking and self-destructive thoughts that these events usually incur - a win-win.

2.8 Relentlessly Attack Your Weakest Link

We are supposed to fear everything that could hurt us. It is our inner chimp doing what it is hardwired to do; keep us from discomfort. But in an age where our fears are more psychological than physical, it tends to hinder more than it helps. Of course, we shouldn't seek to eliminate this sense of fear, after all there may be occasions where it does indeed keep us from harm. But with time and experience we can learn to override the chimp when our fears are not actually life-threatening but still prevent us from leaving our comfort zones.

Your fears and weaknesses, whatever they may be, conscious or subconscious, are the weakest links in your life, holding you back from reaching your full potential. For those who want to win a triathlon, but struggle with swimming, swimming is your weak link. For those who want to start a business, but struggle with accounting, this too will create your weakest link. Your time must therefore be prioritized in dealing with these weakest links. Anything else, although potentially beneficial, is not the most efficient use of your time. You can build a racecar with the best engine, brakes and suspension in the field, but if the weakest link is neglected, such as tires, the car cannot utilize these upgrades and the effort from upgrading all other components was essentially wasted.

It is no good trying to circumvent weak links either, as I see many attempt. No amount of exercise will see you lose weight if you consume more calories than you burn. Even if you can find ways around them, they will always come back to haunt you at some point. There is only one true way to remove your weakest links and that is to completely eliminate them. And the most efficient way to eliminate them is to attack them relentlessly. This may sound dramatic, but the drama is purposeful. You cannot timidly attempt to address weak links as you will almost certainly fail. They are your weakest link for a reason; they fill you with fear and dread. You need the aggression, passion and mentally of attack to overcome the fear and uncertainty, much like how we should make ourselves as big, loud and intimidating as possible to scare off a bear, as opposed to gently wishing it away. You need to have the mindset of total annihilation.

Grant Cardone applies a 10x rule when it comes to sales. For example, to make 10 sales, you should pitch to ten times this amount (100 people). For three new job hires you should look to interview 30 candidates. The same principle can also be applied to our weakest links. If swimming is your weak point, you need to get as many hours swimming as practically possible. If accounting is your weakness, take online courses, watch videos, read about it incessantly until you can do it in your sleep. If you want to get into that top university, but your math is borderline, attack math relentlessly and do as many practice problems as possible. Prioritize it over all other work if possible. Get a tutor, watch online videos, do hundreds of examples and problems. Relentlessly attack your weakest link until it is no longer your weakest.

For whatever reason I once had an irrational fear of talking over the phone. Face to face conversations were no problem, but calling on the phone reduced me to a mumbling mess. My words would jumble and I would become incoherent. This is a problem in the construction industry, where information moves rapidly and misinformation can end up costing fortunes. I tended to put off calling until the very last moment where I absolutely had to. Unfortunately, this point was often too late, and in the end, communication became my weakest link and reduced my competence as an engineer. Driven mostly by pure frustration (incidentally a great motivator) I countered this by making as many phone calls as possible whenever I could. When sending an email, I would call first, even if it wasn't necessary. I even called manufacturers about random questions for products we were using. I wasn't directly calling about the product, I could probably find the question in the product literature, I was calling because

I was frustrated with my lack of telephone skills and I needed to relentlessly attack my weakest link. The issue soon disappeared; I had no problem communicating over the phone. What's more, people were calling me more often as my newfound communication skills instilled confidence in others. I was then able to move on to my next weakest link. And here the magic lies.

By constantly chasing our weakest links, we continuously keep improving. Once you have overcome your current weakness, and it ceases to be your weakest link, you can reap the reward and move on to the next weakest. This mentality drives a continuous cycle of improvement, building competence with each iteration. The second you stop chasing your weaknesses you stagnate. But in a competitive word where the competition never idles, whether it be colleagues or business rivals, even standing still can be seen as backwards progress.

The idea of continually attacking your weakest link also corresponds with the Pareto principle, which states that, for many events, roughly 80 percent of the results comes from just 20 percent of the work. Your weakest link, being your largest point of failure, is certainly contained within this 20 percent of most important work you could be doing. It will therefore also be the work which reaps 80 percent of the results.

Your weakest link needs to become your priority, and where most of your time should be dedicated. It needs to be addressed as soon as possible. Every day it is postponed encourages the fear to grow, making it increasingly more difficult to finally address, much like how the anticipation of a bungee jump is usually worse than the jump itself. The longer you fear something, the more daunting it appears when you are finally forced to confront it. The longer you stand at the top of that bungee jump looking down over the edge, the more likely it is that fear will overcome you, and every second you delay increases the chance of abandoning the jump altogether. When I first moved away from home, I was dreading what was to come. Dwelling on this for weeks allowed this fear to multiply until I nearly aborted the idea altogether. Upon actually doing it, however, it wasn't half as bad as I thought. The thought was worse than the action.

Attacking your weakest links does require you to be able to honestly and accurately identify them, however. In most cases this will be evident; it is usually identified as the task you hate performing the most or that fills you with the most dread. Perhaps this could be cold calling or public speaking. It could be measured in terms of performance, such as your lowest grade in class or the largest area of improvement in a job performance assessment. If you are still struggling, sit down and write down a list of the areas you think are most likely to be impacting your progress. Which one fills you with the most dread or discomfort? Which one would you like to improve the most? Narrow the list by identifying which weak links would most likely increase your performance by the greatest amount if it were no longer a problem. Then develop a plan for attacking it relentlessly until it is no longer an issue.

To improve how we address our fears and weaknesses, we need to get used to being uncomfortable and forcing ourselves outside our comfort zones. A large part of this is expanding our comfort zone so less tasks fall outside it altogether. This is achieved purely through exposure time and repetition. We stare the scary monster in the face long enough for it to no longer be scary. Just like how driving once used to induce fear as a learner, for it to suddenly become a mundane and thoughtless task, so too can any fear outside your comfort zone. Constant exposure, and the mental resilience it builds, is the most efficient way.

Task:

For the most efficient use of time, we need to focus on the 20 percent of work that yields 80 percent of the results. In terms of self-development, this means prioritizing your weakest links and attacking them aggressively and relentlessly until they are no longer your weakest.

This becomes an iterative cycle. Once the issue is no longer the weakest link, reap the reward and move straight onto the next. This mentality will become ingrained over time, as you see the results and transformations firsthand. Soon you will find yourself much more productive, enabling you to achieve your goals in less time and with much less discomfort.

2.9 Build Mental Resilience by Seeking Fear

There is perhaps no greater irony than the fact that the biggest obstacles preventing us from reaching our full potential reside within us. Indeed, we are often our own worst enemies. Despite the immense physical restrictions life can force upon us, from growing up in an abusive household to being born into destitute poverty, our greatest shackles lie within our subconscious. The irony deepens further with the realization that our chimp, the part of the brain that was developed to ensure our survival, often hinders us from thriving. We can learn to manage the chimp as we have seen before, but the ability to do this requires practice. To master our emotions, and therefore our mental resilience, we must actively seek experiences of short-term discomfort by purposely placing ourselves in uncomfortable situations. By doing so we can start to build a tolerance for discomfort, in turn reducing our chances of succumbing to it.

There are few who better display this mental aptitude for building mental resilience through actively seeking pain than retired Navy Seal and ultra-runner David Goggins. David Goggins is the personification of grit. Although I have been seeking to build my mental resilience since my mid-twenties, Goggins' bestselling book "Can't Hurt Me" highlighted the fact that the mind and body can withstand much more than most could even imagine possible. David takes tackling your weakest links to a whole new level. Not only did he go through Hell Week, one of the most intensive military training programs, three times to become a U.S. Navy SEAL (with two fractured legs), he also took to ultra-running, finishing a dizzying 135-mile race through Death Valley in the middle of summer for 32 hours straight. He also performed 1000 pull-ups every morning before breakfast on route to breaking the record of 4030 pullups achieved in 17 hours. All this without realizing that he had a hole in his heart which reduced his aerobic capacity.

Goggins built this incredible mental fortitude through what he coins "callusing" the mind. Boxers, for example, develop great tolerances against getting punched in the head that would knock most out instantly. When training for the pull-up record, the strain on his skin from the friction of the bar created large solid calluses on his palms. These protected his palm by hardening his skin to stop it from tearing. He applied the same principle to his mind. When creating mental friction by going against the mind's constant need for comfort, you can gradually callous over your fear of discomfort and increase your mental pain tolerance. The event doesn't become any less discomforting, but you are better able to deal with the discomfort.

To callus your mind and start building a fierce mental resilience, start actively seeking discomfort to allow these mental calluses to form. Modern life tends to be comfortable for the majority in the western world. We wake up, grab a coffee, go to work, come back, eat dinner, watch TV for a couple of hours, and then go to bed. The most difficult choice for some is what sort of milk to put in their frappuccinos. This means we have to actively seek situations we know will make us uncomfortable. Is it raining outside? Go for an uncomfortably wet run. Had a long Friday at the office and see everyone else leaving for the weekend? Stay behind and do 30 minutes of extra uncomfortable work. Perhaps wake up to an uncomfortably cold shower. Do whatever it takes to seek discomfort. Gradually your tolerance for pain will increase and what used to bother you before will seem trivial. With each memory of overcoming discomfort, your mind will become increasingly hardened.

Every time you successfully push through your mental barriers you build upon this resilience. By seeking discomfort, you are not a masochist, as you are not supposed to enjoy these experiences, you are starting to build tolerances against the constant need to give up when discomfort starts to arise. You are simply raising the bar where your chimp feels uncomfortable.

What is lost in Goggins' book, however, is a key component for all successful people that are overlooked; the countless repetitions and hours one spends building these traits. They are rarely mentioned in books because it is unglamorous and doesn't sell. But time and experience are the only guaranteed means of self-improvement. To start building this resistance and avoid falling victim to your chimp's urge for instant gratification, you need to gather experience in overcoming these urges to as large a degree as possible. It is a skill like any other and needs to be practiced with consistency. It needs to be a part of your daily schedule.

This discomfort seeking mentality should be a part of your life forever. There is no endpoint as there is no finite limit for mental resilience. We can always be stronger. We shouldn't fear a life of pain seeking, however. Eventually, the reward from witnessing your mental resilience increase will motivate you, and the feats it enables to be accomplished will far outweigh the temporary pain. Whilst the discomfort will never cease, you will soon learn to better tolerate it. It doesn't become any less painful, but the pain becomes more familiar and, because you have already proved you are capable of pushing through pain, the fear of pain becomes less intense. Furthermore, you will build a vast collection of past successes where you pushed yourself through pain barriers, enabling you to draw upon them for an extra boost of willpower in moments of weakness. When confronted with an uncomfortable situation, you will find yourself less overwhelmed by what is to come. You will procrastinate less and get the job done as best you can with as little mental resistance as possible.

In his book, David explains the 40 percent rule he discovered after the continual completion of feats that he thought were previously beyond him. When your mind first tells you you're done, the point where you are first tempted to stop, you're only 40 percent done. Once you learn this about yourself, you'll soon come to realize that this first point of mental rejection is where you are only just starting to tap into half of what you're capable of. You still have much more to give in reserve. This has even been backed up by scientific studies of athletes who were worked to the first urge to quit. Measurements of the muscles found they were not even close to a point of muscular failure. The urge to stop is most likely the mind trying to prevent the muscles from taking too much damage in the first place. Once again, the mind does everything it can to convince you to avoid discomfort.

To practice pushing past this 40 percent point of failure, aim to work an extra 10 percent past this point where your body and mind first scream for you to stop. If the maximum distance you can run is 10 miles before the urge to stop becomes too great, force yourself to run one further mile. Over time, and with continual success at giving this extra 10 percent, you will notice your tolerance for discomfort greatly expands. One of the best ways to practice this is through physical activities.

Unfortunately, there is no shortcut to experience. As Goggins quotes "it takes 20 years to build 20 years of experience". Make it a habit to perform one task every day and add it to your habit table. Seek an activity, whether it be physical or mental, that takes you 10 percent past your self-imposed maximum. The reward for this will be unlocking performance beyond 90 percent of the population.

Task:

Add the habit "perform uncomfortable task" to your daily habit table. Create a list of activities that will allow you to perform this habit every day. Physical feats are always a good way of finding mental limits as they challenge the mind in a more primal manner where the chimp often reacts explosively.

Whenever your mind and body first scream at you to give in, force an extra 10 percent of performance before you stop. If you find yourself too bored to work after 60 minutes, where you would normally quit and go for a coffee break, lock yourself in the room, and work an extra 6 minutes. Although uncomfortable, these are small sacrifices towards developing greater mental resilience, a trait that allows us to accomplish more than our minds would ever lead us to believe.

3. Social Skills

3.1 Maintain a Positive Outlook

The power of positive thinking may be cliché, but it is a very real and immensely underappreciated phenomenon. How happy or content we feel at any given moment is often a manifestation of our deeper mental outlook on life. The conscious and subconscious brain are far more powerful than most appreciate. They are also highly synergistic; one exerts tremendous influence on the other. We cannot control our subconscious, but we can control our conscious thoughts. By actively avoiding negative conscious thoughts, and instead replacing them with positive ones, we can encourage the subconscious to also think in this more positive manner.

You cannot be positive all the time. In fact, it is technically impossible. You cannot define positivity without negativity, much like you cannot label something as hot or cold if everything's the same temperature. Negativity is therefore an inevitability. So, creating a positive outlook involves not only avoiding negativity as far as possible, but also how we choose to respond to it once it does present itself.

Unsurprisingly, positive people are most likely to get positive results. They tend to persevere easier through tough events, communicate and socialize better and succumb less to stress and anxiety. Whilst some are fortunate enough to be born with a greater propensity for positivity, others must work harder towards it. Like anything else, however, it is a skill which can be improved with time and experience, so long as we understand why negativity arises and we realize when it first starts to infect us.

Whilst easy to put into words, mitigating negativity is no easy feat. Negativity is like a virus; once it is introduced it can spread rapidly beyond control. Studies have found an interesting concept called the "negativity bias" which demonstrates just how dominating negative thinking can truly be. The negative bias is our tendency to not only register negative stimuli more readily than positive ones but also our tendency to dwell on these events for extended periods of time. Also known as positive-negative asymmetry, this negativity bias means that we feel the sting of a rebuke much more than we would feel joy from praise. Your boss criticizing your work, for example, instils much more emotion than the same person praising it. Criticisms often have a greater impact than compliments and bad news frequently draws more attention than good. This negativity bias can have a detrimental effect on behavior, decisions, and even relationships.

Research suggests that this negativity bias first starts to emerge in infancy. Very young children tend to pay greater attention to positive facial expressions and tone of voice, but this begins to shift as they near one year of age with brain studies indicating that babies begin to experience greater brain responses to negative stimuli during the latter half of a child's first year of life.

Another study conducted by psychologist John Cacioppo showed participants pictures of either positive, negative, or neutral images. The researchers then observed electrical activity in the brain. Negative images produced a much stronger response in the cerebral cortex than that of positive or neutral images, further highlighting the asymmetric influence of negative emotions on the brain.

Due to a surge in activity in the critical information processing area of the brain, our behaviors and attitudes tend to be influenced to a greater degree by negative experiences, likely a chemical result of evolution. Earlier in human history, paying attention to dangerous threats was literally a matter of life and death. Those who were more attuned to danger, and who paid greater attention to potential negative situations, were more likely to survive. Positive thoughts on the other hand, although they make us feel good, do not offer practical survival advantages.

Through survival of the fittest, those more aware of dangers were more likely to survive and pass down genes responsible for the inherent negativity bias. Evolution suggests that this tendency to dwell on the negative more than the positive is simply a way for our subconscious to keep us from harm. The greater we fear something, the more likely we are to distance ourselves from it. Whilst this defense mechanism was once essential for survival, modern day scenarios often render it more of a hindrance. Evolution has not kept pace with societal developments, and our chimp cannot distinguish between historic threats against surviving and modern threats against thriving.

Our mental outlook has a significant effect on our physiology. Positive thoughts release dopamine, a mood elevator, whereas negative thoughts produce cortisol, a mood killer. When hit by a negative thought, the brain releases cortisol as an alarm system to warn of potential dangers. Unfortunately, the brain cannot distinguish between events which pose a genuine threat to survival, such as avoiding a car crash, and those which do not, such as receiving a snide email. As a result, both events can release similar levels of cortisol, and whilst cortisol may help avoid a car crash, it most likely won't help in delicately responding to an obnoxious message.

Neuroscientists Mark Waldman and Andrew Newberg successfully identified the physical effects of the negativity bias on the brain by placing patients into an fMRI scanner—a huge donut-shaped magnet that can record neural changes occurring in the brain - and flashed the word "NO" in front of them for less than a second. Neurological changes in the brain were quickly witnessed with dozens of stress-producing hormones and neurotransmitters released. These chemicals immediately interrupted the normal functioning of the brain, impairing logic, reasoning, language processing, and communication. The word "NO", even when flashed for tenths of a second, with no other context, was found to increase feelings of anxiety and depression, especially for those already predisposed to such emotions. Other studies repeating similar experiments were also found to damage key structures that regulate mental functions of the brain including memory, feelings, and emotions.

Any form of negative rumination - for example, worrying about embarrassing yourself or how you will cope in a new social situation - stimulates the release of these destructive neurochemicals. The more negative thoughts circulating in your mind, therefore, the more likely you are to experience emotional turmoil. Fortunately, this also works in reverse, where focusing on positive thoughts promotes chemicals that elevate your mood.

Perhaps the most dangerous aspect of negative thinking, however, is its virality. Like a virus, negativity, if left untreated, spreads until it completely consumes its host. It is also extremely contagious; one person's negative attitude can spread to others through the same manner as how observing the word no, with no other context, changes the neurology of the brain. Our subconscious picks up other's negative attitudes and recognizes that if this person feels threatened, maybe we should too. Hence why spending time with negative people can induce feelings of negativity within us, even if there is no tangible threat.

Unfortunately, avoiding negative thoughts is no easy feat since humans are so inherently predisposed to them. In fact, you may have noticed that this whole chapter has so far focused on avoiding negative thoughts as opposed to promoting positive ones. While I could have framed the text above in terms of the benefits of positive thinking, as opposed to the dangers of negative thinking, it wouldn't have carried so much weight. We are all wired to pay greater attention to the negatives.

Mindfulness, an act advocated numerous times throughout this book, is the best first step in combating negativity. Understand that negative thoughts and reactions are invoked by the chimp through a primal biological mechanism to keep us from danger. We cannot actively control this subconscious mechanism, so we therefore cannot be defined by it. But we must remain mindful and vigilant of when these negative thoughts start to affect our actions, of which we are fully responsible for.

When first overwhelmed by negative thoughts, ask yourself whether the situation at hand really is a threat to personal survival, or whether it is more likely to be your primal safety mechanism at play. For example, you are asked to give a presentation in front of senior managers. Whilst the thought of such an event would send most chimps into overdrive, mindfulness can help to take a step back and evaluate the situation. The threat to personal safety is obviously not present, instead it is our chimp not being able to distinguish between the two types of threats; threats against surviving and threats against thriving. We are not in control of our chimp, so these reactions are inevitable and we shouldn't be judged by them. All we can control, and therefore all we should focus on, is deciding how we act upon them. The simple act of being mindful is often enough to significantly stem the flow of negative thoughts and prevent them from spreading - like a virus - until they fully consume you.

Once mindful of the fact that negative thoughts are inevitable and merely the result of the chimp's lack of ability to identify threats as anything other than a physical danger, the situation can then be consciously reframed to instead focus on whatever positive outcomes might emerge. The negativity bias ensures we think of all worst-case scenarios, such as fumbling your words or embarrassing yourself, but rarely of potential positives, such as establishing your name and competence with senior management. Remember, behind every error and failure lies a learning opportunity. If you do fail, your failure will enable you to become a better presenter next time. Although one cannot simply wish away negative thoughts - they are far too powerful to simply ignore - consciously thinking about the positives will offset the intensity of any negatives. This allows for a sense of grounding where you can stop the runaway train of negative thinking and instead build up by highlighting the positives.

One of the best examples I have come across in understanding the power of positive thinking comes from the unlikeliest of sources. I once had a conversation with someone who had spent a fair amount of his life in prison. He was forced to learn the power of positive thinking in order to survive the ordeal. He recalled his stint as being the toughest and most negative period of his life, having lost everything; his job, his family and his friends. Yet in prison, negative thoughts and actions, such as social seclusion and crying, make you appear weak and hence a victim. He recalls that new inmates who appear weak are the first to be extorted for money or worse. You have to make yourself appear in control, no matter what the realities inside your mind are. Whenever he went to sleep, he would lay down and go through all the things he was thankful for. He looked at other inmates and was thankful for still having all his limbs, his sight and the fact that each night got him one day closer to release. He had to think positively; it was purely a survival mechanism to keep from danger in much the same way that chimpanzees try their utmost to hide pain when injured for fear of the rest of the troop leaving them behind. The strongest in jail have to fake it at first, everything is about image. Eventually your subconscious mind falls in line with your conscious thoughts and you adapt. There certainly is some truth in the saying "fake it till you make it". Ironically, he had to endure the most negative moments of his life to become the strong positive person he is today. He says he doesn't let things like feelings or bad moods control him anymore. He now controls them by actively thinking positively in order to displace any negativity.

Whilst positive thinking is an internal affair of the mind, we can mitigate the effects of negative thinking through certain external factors. First, try to spend more time around positive people and less with those who are perpetually negative. Negativity is highly contagious and the thoughts of others can exert significant influence on us. Often it is not completely viable to distance completely from negative people - we cannot simply ignore family, friends or colleagues whom we are forced to regularly converse with. But be mindful of the influence these people can have on you and ensure you distance yourself mentally when others begin to exude negative thoughts. By consciously avoiding negativity our subconscious stands a much better chance at avoiding it too.

When dealing with these perpetually negative people, try to displace their negativity with thoughts of positivity. Consider yourself the light in their lives and show them a positive outlook which they may have never considered. This challenge has become somewhat of a guilty pleasure for me. Whenever I come across someone with negative thoughts, such as gossiping or complaining, I subtly play a harmless game to try and switch their attitude. For example, they might complain of how much work their boss has placed upon them and how unfair it is. I will then attempt to flip their view by telling them that their boss must clearly think very highly of them since they've been solely trusted with so much important work. Their mood immediately flips. Similarly, when someone starts to complain about others behind their back, I like to draw attention to more positive aspects of the person being complained about. To some this may seem slightly patronizing, but to me it is a way to avoid succumbing to others' contagious negativity.

A negative person and their thoughts can be compared to a spider and its web. The more time spent in the presence of someone's negative thoughts, the more likely you are to become stuck in their web, as their negative projections start to induce negative thoughts of your own by association. Once stuck in this web it is almost impossible to break free no matter how hard you wriggle. Eventually, once weakened and exhausted, the spider will move in and consume you.

The best way to avoid this entrapment is to keep a safe distance from others' negative web altogether. This doesn't necessarily mean avoiding contact with others at all costs, but rather, keep a mental distance by being mindful of when the negative thoughts of others could start to influence your own. Feel free to converse with them as you deem necessary, but avoid participating and becoming sucked into a toxic way of thinking. Remain amiable but distant. Try to introduce positivity as mentioned above but be prepared to leave a toxic conversation as soon the opportunity arises.

A large component of maintaining a positive outlook involves being prepared to let small injustices go. You have to know when to cut to your losses, even if you are in the right. Road rage is a prime example. When that pickup truck rides your rear, just move over and let them go. It can be incredibly difficult to back down, especially among the more competitive of us, for fear of appearing weak, but there is no benefit in engaging with these toxic people. Remember, they are a spider, and as soon as you allow yourself to be influenced by their toxic behavior you risk becoming trapped in their web. In fact, it takes a higher level of mental awareness and courage to actively avoid these traps and recognize that there is nothing of value to be gained by engaging. Many businesses fail because so much of their time is consumed by chasing small injustices, such as a low value invoice left unpaid, when they could be dedicating their time towards acquiring better opportunities of much greater value.

A positive attitude also requires avoiding the pitfalls of jealousy and envy. It is common for many to resent others for their success, especially when it is at their expense. I have already spoken of the time I was passed over for a promotion where the job was awarded to a younger, less experienced colleague. I am ashamed to admit I resented him a little for it, even though his better aptitude for work meant he deserved it far more than I did. I wasn't as friendly as I should have been and didn't congratulate him on his well-deserved promotion. My thoughts became toxic until it consumed my entire attitude for days. Most would have had moments like this to some degree, after all it is the chimp who subconsciously pushes these thoughts onto you without your immediate control. Perhaps a friend has just bought a house while you're still struggling to pay rent. A wave of envy consumes you and you seek to discourage them by reminding them that they were lucky to have help from their parents, or how big their mortgage must be. Now both of you feel unpleasant. Maybe a friend has made the brave decision to start a business and you go out of your way to remind them how 50 percent of all businesses fail by their fifth year. We are envious that they may be on the road to a more lucrative future than us and that arouses feelings of insecurity which we try to push onto them. It is perfectly reasonable to feel jealous; it is the chimp expressing its discomfort with our own lives.

But we are not defined by these inevitable thoughts, just on how we choose to act upon them. You may feel envious, but express positivity by congratulating them on their success. You won't change your fortunes by bringing down others, only by raising yourself up. Not only do you stem the flow of negative thoughts before they have time to consume you, but quite often you will find this positivity won't go unnoticed by the other person. This is easier said than done, and sometimes the pain of missing out is too raw to be happy about, but at the very least don't go out of your way to discourage someone else from their success. Nothing good will come of it and it is a loser's mentality.

On a final note regarding negativity, one must be extremely cautious of gossiping. Gossip, the staple of any office, hair salon or watercooler, is a breeding ground for toxic behavior where it is easy to fall victim to others' poor mentalities.

Studies suggest people spend up to 80 percent of their conversational time gossiping. It is a normal and unavoidable part of socializing where the sharing of personal information with others facilitates a more personal sense of communication. It can be thought of as the modern equivalent of grooming, a vital component of social bonding for animals during downtimes.

Gossiping itself is not necessarily the problem, nor does it always have to be negative. For example, we can gossip about how well someone is looking or how many sales they made last quarter. A 2019 meta-analysis published in the journal Social Psychological and Personality Science found that, of the 52 minutes a day the 467 participants spent on average gossiping, 75 percent of this was neutral.

Just 15 percent of the conversations analyzed were deemed negative. So, while it is true that people can spend a significant amount of time talking about their peers, oftentimes the chatter is benign. Interestingly, the negativity bias was found in this study as positive gossip amounted to a smaller proportion of just 9 percent.

I am not advocating to avoid all gossip, but rather to engage tastefully. The trick about gossip is, it should give the subject the benefit of the doubt and come from a place of curiosity, not superiority. Engage in gossip to build others up rather than put them down. Remember that gossip travels fast and be prepared for whatever you say to be gossiped by others. If you don't wish for the person whom you're talking about to ever know what you said, then simply don't say it. Assume everything you say will be relayed back to that person. I have found that those who complain about others behind their back are often subject to the same treatment. I personally live by the ethos that others complain of you as much as you complain of others. It is hard to badmouth someone who you trust would never do the same to you. In other words, you reap what you sow.

Task:

Catching negativity before it affects your mood is extremely difficult in the heat of the moment. To begin, however, make a list of the negative activities in recent memory that dwelled within you and affected your mood. Think about how they ruined the rest of your day when they needn't. This could be anything, engaging with an aggressive driver, an uncomplimentary email or simply being in the presence of others' negativity.

In 90 percent of these scenarios, continued negativity offered no benefit and should have been eliminated before it started to dominate your thoughts. Think about how you could have avoided it in the first place. For a snide email, you could have walked away and relaxed with a coffee for 10 minutes to let the chimp vent. You may feel good in the moment for having stuck up for yourself, but this is often followed by feelings of guilt, even if you know you were in the right.

From this point on, try to be as mindful as possible of any future events where you feel negative thoughts start to influence your thoughts and actions. Be wary of spiders when they are trying to trap you in their negativity web and either try to steer the conversation in a more positive direction or discreetly distance yourself from it altogether, physically or mentally. Let the small things go, even if you know you were in the right.

3.2 Be Liberal with Benefit of the Doubt

This chapter is an extension to the previous, but so important I thought I would delve a little deeper. A major component of building a more positive mindset is to first prevent negative thoughts from entering it. A major source of negativity stems from small encounters with others, whether someone swerves in front of us while driving or criticizes our work. Even a brief encounter of just a few seconds with someone negative can flip our mood for the rest of the day, such is the toxicity of negativity.

Humans are very quick to judge others. Mankind has relied on this immediate reaction to survive for thousands of years. In past ages of fight or flight, identifying whether something is friend or foe in just a split second can often mean the difference between life and death. Yet in a complex modern age of impersonal communication mediums such as email and texting, communications are easily misinterpreted by both sender and receiver, even if there was no original intent of offense. Human judgment, by nature, is black and white. Anything in between these two extremes is ambiguous, which frustrates our chimp who must know if something is a threat or not. Our chimp seeks to avoid this frustration by manufacturing perceptions of others as best it can with the limited information available in order to draw its own conclusion and avoid ambiguity of potential threats. Unfortunately, this information is usually not accurate enough to make a fair judgment.

Anti-vaxxers are a prime example of this black and white mechanism. A Texas Tech University study surveyed 158 participants to rate the likelihood of mortality-related events. Whilst anti-vaxxers believe that vaccine-related death or injury is likely, what researchers also found was that these same skeptics overestimated the possibility of death by other negative events, such as from fireworks and flooding. In a second experiment, the same participants were then asked to rate the likelihood of neutral or positive events. Researchers found that those who were skeptical of vaccines proved more accurate in identifying positive or neutral likelihoods, inferring that anti-vaxxers tend to overestimate the likelihood of negative events but not positive or neutral ones. We already know this as the negativity bias, but it shows the primal need for clear cut answers. The limbic system struggles to accept the fact that although science has proved vaccines safe, there is still an element of doubt, no matter how small. But it is this little bit of doubt that confuses the chimp and, in a bid to draw its own conclusive answer, categorizes all vaccines as a potential threat. Unfortunately, this same principle also applies to the judgment of others.

There are two types of judgments we draw of others' behavior: situational and personal. When we make situational judgments, we believe their behavior is due to external factors regarding their current situation. For example, a coworker might have been impatient with you because they are tired, overworked, or have family issues that are leaching into their work life. But we know this person to be generally pleasant, so the cause of this behavior is likely due to external factors such as stress. Personality attributions, on the other hand, deal with a person's character. If this same person is always short-tempered, it is perhaps an issue with their character and internal values.

Our chimp, who is responsible for split-second judgments, is notably poor at distinguishing between these two types of judgments. Firstly, there is often too little context to make a fair judgment, especially if we do not know much about the person. Our limbic system deals only with definitives; if we do not have enough information to make a situational judgment, we, therefore, resort to making a personal judgment. This might sound unfair, and to a large degree it is, but remember our chimp thinks only in terms of black and white and must determine whether someone is a potential threat or not.

Anything in between will most likely be categorized as a threat as the chimp does not take risks when it comes to survival.

As a result, we often judge others poorly. Just recently I visited the very first Starbucks in Seattle. Being accustomed to simply walking in and queuing at the counter to place my order, I walked in without realizing there was an outside queue to enter this historic landmark. I was swiftly scolded by the lady in the front of the queue about how ignorant I was and I needed to get my behind to the back of the queue like everyone else (she chose more colorful words, however). The mistake was genuine; I simply hadn't realized there was a queue because I was not expecting it. I should have been judged on the situation, but she judged me on a personal level. She taught me a valuable lesson, however, to try to understand a person's situation before making a personal judgment.

Misjudging others is not only unfair, but it is also extremely wasteful. When we judge others as negative, we tend to distance ourselves from them and avoid building any form of relationship. We therefore miss out on potential opportunities such as friendships, strong working relationships, or other information that might have benefitted us. By judging others and closing our minds to them, we miss out on potential opportunities.

In order to avoid jumping straight to making personal judgments, and therefore miss out on potential opportunities and fruitful relationships, I use a firm, but fair rule, called the "one free pass" rule. As long as the person in question has not significantly impacted me, I give them a free pass when they wrong me before I judge that person's character. I assume whatever wrong was committed was because of a situational factor as opposed to a personal one. As Elon Musk once quipped "people should give other people the benefit of the doubt until proven otherwise". This does not mean to trust people blindly, but it's often better to give people the benefit of the doubt rather than being constantly cynical about others' motives. If you don't truly know someone, you should refrain from judging their personality until you know more about their situation.

This technique removes a huge source of burden. Slamming the horn when a motorist swerves in front you will unleash a tidal wave of negative thoughts and energy within you. Even though it was not your fault, you still feel terrible for losing your cool. Instead, we should assume this person made a situational mistake and give them a free pass. This helps not only avoid all those toxic thoughts, but it may just help someone else who desperately needs it. I try to imagine myself in their position; there have been times when I have driven around in new areas trying to find a new location when I accidentally cut someone off or forget to indicate. Although it was my fault for being distracted, there was no intent to offend. Every time I now come across a questionable motorist, I give them one free pass. Perhaps they too are lost or have other events weighing on their mind. No man should judge unless he asks himself in absolute honesty whether, in a similar situation, he might not have done the same. Until you know their situation, it is not fair to judge their integrity.

Whenever this particular topic comes up, I always think back to a past colleague who suffered for many years with debilitating back pain. At age 18, she was in the passenger seat of a friend's car that was broadsided by a drunk driver traveling at great speed. The passenger door where she was sitting was the direct point of impact, resulting in a shattered pelvis and two cracked vertebrae. It took dozens of titanium screws, plates, pins, and hours of surgery to reconstruct and stabilize her pelvis and lower back. Due to a previously unknown/undiagnosed autoimmune issue, her body then began to reject the metal used to piece her hip back together, compounding the misery of the incident. It took years of medical intervention, physical therapy, pain, tears, and willpower to recover to a point where she could walk again.

When parking up at a gas station one sunny afternoon, she parked in the handicapped space and presented her blue disabled placard as she is entitled to do. A gentleman, rather disgruntled with the fact that two seemingly abled bodies had misused the disabled parking space, lambasted us with some of the most vulgar abuse I had ever witnessed. Although my friend was often bedbound with crippling pain for days at a time, she was unfairly judged within just a few seconds by someone who knew nothing of her extreme situation. Although a harrowing experience, I did learn something rather valuable that I have since tried to apply to my everyday life; if we don't have enough information to judge someone with absolute certainty, give them a free pass and move on for both your sakes.

3.3 You Can Rarely Win an Argument… Even When You're Right.

This chapter comes straight from Dale Carnegie's masterpiece book "How to Win Friends and Influence People". I am shamelessly ripping off Mr. Carnegie's legendary writings because this knowledge has had such a profound effect on my life. Almost daily I find myself in contact with someone who has an opposite agenda to mine, whether it be settling cost differences, selling a product or service, or simply trying to convince my partner they are perhaps in the wrong. Incidentally, this tip may prove to be the greatest tip towards a successful marriage.

Even if you know you are right, you can still easily lose an argument. Although counterintuitive, Dale Carnegie explains this concisely in his book:

"Nine times out of ten, an argument ends with each of the contestants more firmly convinced than ever that he is absolutely right. You can't win an argument. You can't because if you lose it, you lose it; and if you win it, you lose it. Why? Well, suppose you triumph over the other man and shoot his argument full of holes and prove that he is non compos mentis. Then what? You will feel fine. But what about him? You have made him feel inferior. You have hurt his pride. He will resent your triumph. And - "A man convinced against his will is of the same opinion still."

The above passage can be combined with the phrase "you may have won the battle, but you haven't won the war". You may be able to brute force your way through an argument by shutting the opponent down with irrefutable logic and facts. But this "win" is short-term. Longer-term, you will have likely burned bridges and lost out on any future opportunities a healthy relationship might have presented. Healthy long-term relationships are usually more profitable than short-term gains. This is why cell phone providers are often willing to discount the first few months of a new plan; they are willing to forgo immediate profits in the belief of greater future returns. So, by burning bridges, more often than not we lose overall. Retailers such as Costco, who are renowned for their customer service, are willing to return items even if they're not obliged to because they see greater value in future customers over the immediate profit from not returning the item. This applies most appropriately in any context where the relationship is ongoing – such as family, partners, friends, work colleagues, and superiors. In other words, most personal or professional contexts benefit from strong long-term relationships.

Dale Carnegie defines this as losing someone's goodwill. "As wise old Ben Franklin used to say: if you argue and rankle and contradict, you may achieve a victory sometimes, but it will be an empty victory because you will never get your opponent's goodwill."

Why do most people, no matter how intelligent, keep arguing even though they know they are in the wrong? It once again boils down to primal tendencies and our inability to recognize them. The chimp values its sense of pride above all facts and logic. Your chimp does not care whether you are technically correct or not, all it cares about is avoiding potential dangers in order to survive. When someone challenges your argument, it is not logic that is the problem, but rather the chimp's pride. When challenged, the chimp perceives this as a threat. If it begins to feel inferior, as it will do if the other person gets an upper hand in an argument, the chimp views this as a predatory danger. The chimp cannot distinguish between a threat to pride from a verbal debate and a threat from a potential predator. The chimp views all contexts as black and white, and a threat of any kind means only one thing; potential for harm. To avoid this danger, therefore, the chimp must argue, not to be factually correct, but to maintain its pride and to not be seen as inferior and therefore easy prey. Again, it is a primal defense mechanism that is not suitable for modern-day life.

Pride can drive even the most rational of people to argue about such seemingly irrational topics; it is a primal trait that still dominates many of our decisions. You may be correct technically, but if you are trying to argue against someone's emotional chimp, trying to win them round to your way of thinking will be just as futile as if you were wrong.

Instead, we have to avoid confronting the chimp and instead engage with the rational human part of the brain. We cannot tell someone they are wrong, even if they are, for fear of upsetting their chimp who will flip into a fight or flight response and argue, not to be factually correct, but to not appear weak, and therefore in danger. The skill in arguing, therefore, lies in the ability to convince the other's chimp that they are in a safe environment where there is no threat to safety. We do this by making their chimp feel valued.

The key to successfully negotiating, and winning people over to your way of thinking, is therefore not wholly dependent on the content of your argument itself, but rather in how you convey this content to the opposing party. Dale Carnegie suggests that the only way to "win" an argument is to avoid it altogether. Instead of trying to force your views onto someone else, encourage them to come to the same conclusion on their own.

A misunderstanding is rarely ended by an argument but rather by tact, diplomacy, and a genuine and sympathetic desire to see the other person's point of view. A key component in achieving this is to simply listen and give your opponent a chance to be heard. Don't interrupt, defend, or debate. Allow the opposing party's chimp to vent and exhaust itself before trying to engage. By listening, and respecting their right to have their opinion heard, whether it be right or wrong, we avoid the chimp feeling a sense of inferiority and danger. Listening makes them feel valued, and as long as the chimp feels valued and not inferior, it won't push back when engaging in more reasonable and logical thoughts.

To aid this, I have learned to use different variations of one main phrase, differing slightly based on context, to disarm an opponent when an argument is approaching; "I may be wrong, I often can be, but I thought .... Let's look that up". Admitting you may be wrong is the ultimate way to disarm an opponent in an argument. Never say "you're wrong" even if they are indeed wrong. Incidentally, you can say "you're wrong" in more ways than simple speech; intonation, gestures and even looks can give this same impression. "You're wrong" is a surefire way to ensure no future progress will be made at all. Instead, by admitting you may be wrong, your opponent will more often than not feel the need to bring themselves to the same level as you. Now both parties are open-minded and the correct answer is more likely to surface. Furthermore, no chimps are likely to take offense or have their pride hurt.

Salespeople, or at least the ones worth their keep, know this theory intimately. When shopping for a new car, many will enter a dealership having researched other vehicles they are also considering. A common roadblock for salespeople is closing the sale, a time when many customers often say "I'm going to test drive the new Ford before I make my decision". An inexperienced salesperson, trying desperately to close the sale, might try to argue by forcing upon the buyer facts and logic. "You don't want a Ford; it gets less gas mileage and has one year's less warranty. The Ford is an inferior car, instead, our car is far superior". This might all be true, but you have now questioned the buyer's decision and have therefore unwittingly knocked their pride. Now the salesman has to deal with the buyer's emotional chimp, significantly reducing the chance of a sale. Even though the buyer may have had every intention of buying this car, the sheer fact that the salesman challenged their pride may be enough to completely reverse their decision.

A more experienced salesperson, however, knows to never engage in a negotiation with an argument or debate. Instead, they know to use tact, diplomacy, and a sympathetic desire to see the other person's viewpoint. They would first ask why they are thinking about buying a Ford; "The Ford is a fine vehicle, in fact, I know a lot of people who have said great things about it. I know you would be very happy with a Ford but I was wondering what features are making you consider it?". Here, by listening to the buyer's needs and wants, you have made them feel valued and their pride remains intact. The buyer is now disengaged and is in a better position to be persuaded. "Well, I hear Fords are very reliable and get 40 miles to the gallon" the buyer might respond. Here we can begin to reason with the rational human side of the buyer: "The Ford does indeed get an impressive 40 miles per gallon. If mileage is important to you, you will love our vehicle, it gets 45 miles per gallon and has a slightly larger fuel tank than the Ford. We can also offer you an extra year's warranty compared to the Ford, as I know reliability is extremely important to you." Firstly, by listening to the customer and allowing them to speak, not only have you allowed for a feeling of importance and value, but you have also allowed the buyer to do much of the selling for you. The buyer told you exactly what will make him buy this car, which you can use to sell the vehicle. The buyer did all the hard work, all you had to do was listen. Once disengaged and more receptive to alternative points of view, a salesperson is much more likely to close the deal.

There are many other excellent insights provided by Dale Carnegie on this subject for those who are interested. An overview is provided in my free eBook https://jason-strong.ck.page. But the key point here is to be tactful when dealing with opposing points of view. Never tell anyone they are wrong; this engages their chimp and you are now in an emotional argument. You can't win, even if you're technically right. If you find yourself in need of winning others round to your way of thinking, first disarm their chimp by admitting you may be wrong with simple phrases such as "See I thought differently, but I may be wrong, I frequently am, let's look this up." By admitting you might be wrong, the other person can now admit they too may be wrong without letting pride or emotion get in the way. Often, they will try and match your humility. From here you can lay on your persuasion skills.

This tip requires one key skill to master. Listening. Only by genuinely listening to others, can you convince the other person that their opinion is valued and disengage their chimp. Most of the time, the argument is not about the immediate subject, rather it is the need for pride to remain intact. That is why people will argue until they're blue in the face even if you both know they're wrong. The next chapter expands on this by detailing the skill of listening.

3.4 Learn to Listen

"Most people do not listen with the intent to understand; they listen with the intent to reply." - Stephen R. Covey

The value of listening is often misunderstood or simply underappreciated. It forms half the equation for becoming a successful communicator, with the other half relating to speaking. The speaking aspect is often more highly appreciated as it is the most obvious; those who are excellent public speakers are usually viewed as confident and competent communicators. Yet, both halves of the equation - listening and speaking - are just as important as each other in maximizing the efficiency and for communicating. But the act of listening extends far beyond simply hearing the words being spoken. Listening involves facilitating a platform for others to be understood. And it is here where most people ultimately fail.

Successful communicators, those who have mastered the art of listening just as well as the art of speaking, are usually found amongst the higher tiers of businesses and society. Most successful managers, bosses and business leaders, need to understand the wants and needs of their customers and employees and how they can take advantage of these needs to leverage profitability. They also maintain much stronger relationships; better bonds are built between those who have stronger connections, which listening facilitates.

Listening is often deemed a passive ability as opposed to a learnable skill. Yet it is indeed a skill like any other that needs to be learned and practiced. No one is born a more capable communicator; the difference comes from knowledge and experience. Studies have shown that the average person can only remember 50 percent of what they've heard straight after hearing it. Another study has shown that only 10 percent of the initial message communicated can be recalled after 3 days. The reason for these shocking statistics is that most think of listening as a passive process that requires little to no effort. And we know humans are inherently interested in themselves above all others. So, when it comes to listening to others, we tend to zone out and not focus entirely on the other person.

Most do not listen with the intent to understand; they listen with the intent to reply. In other words, we listen to the words without trying to grasp the deeper context and meaning behind them. This is usually because we're focused on our own internal dialogue rather than what the speaker is actually trying to communicate. Other times we don't pay attention because we're distracted or daydreaming – when I am in the middle of writing and my partner asks me a question it usually akes me a little time to clear my mind and engage fully with the conversation. Or we may have a preconceived bias against either the speaker or the topic that closes our minds to what's being said. But most of the time we fail to truly listen because we are too busy trying to formulate an idea or response to what is diverting attention away from truly understanding the speaker.

Listening also doesn't mean sitting in silence until it is your turn to speak. It still involves a to-and-fro conversation but of the kind where it keeps the focus on the other person. The key to becoming a good listener, and therefore communicator, lies in creating a platform for others to speak more freely. When listening, everything you say and do should be focused on allowing the speaker to communicate on a deeper level. This often involves asking lots of questions and creating opportunities for the speaker to expand on their thoughts.

Essential traits for effective listening include receptiveness and open-mindedness. It requires us to not put words in other people's mouths, fill in gaps, or presume to understand the other person fully. It also requires you to put yourself in someone else's position, especially if you disagree with what is being said. You don't have to agree with someone to listen to them, but you have to try and understand where they are coming from and why they have the opinion you disagree with. If you can figure out why someone feels the way that they do, you have a much better chance of understanding them and trying to persuade them otherwise.

The following five components, when used synergistically, will allow you to become a more capable listener:

1.   **Eye contact**. Looking directly at the person who's speaking is a clear way to indicate you're paying attention to them. Looking away, even if you're still listening, will make it seem like you're distracted or not interested. I cannot tell you how many people I see looking at their phone or computer when being spoken to, and there is no ruder way to not listen. Sometimes this is done unwittingly when nervous or shy. Conversely, unbroken eye contact can make others uncomfortable.

2. **Body language**. About 60-75 percent of our communication is non-verbal. Both speaker and listener must ensure their body language facilitates good communication. Crossed arms or not facing the other person squarely infers that you are not 100 percent confident or relaxed. The other person is likely to subconsciously pick up on this, making them uncomfortable by association. Facial expressions are also incredibly important when listening. Nodding, tilting your head, smiling – all of these expressions show a response to what the speaker is saying, indicating a genuine interest in what is being said.

3. **Don't interrupt**. Although it's good to ask questions, try not to interrupt the speaker. Let the person complete his or her thoughts before responding or asking questions. Letting other people finish their thoughts, even when you visibly disagree, shows a level of respect that it is more likely to be reciprocated.

4.   **Ask questions.** Critical listening involves asking questions to delve for deeper understanding. When you ask the speaker a question, it drives the conversation to a more meaningful place and

shows that you're interested in understanding the issues. This is a more active form of listening where you are speaking to facilitate greater understanding. Ensure questions are appropriately timed and do not interrupt the speaker.

5.   **Paraphrasing** is also a more active type of listening. When you restate, in your own words, what the speaker is saying, you prove that you're listening carefully and that you are making a great effort to thoroughly understand their view. The speaker feels valued and the conversation is therefore more rewarding for both parties.

Conversations become much trickier when it involves differing opinions. Unfortunately, these controversial conversations are often unavoidable, whether negotiating a salary raise, interviewing for a new job, or expressing a different opinion at work. When people have opposing views to their own, it is easy to criticize and dismiss their opinion as unworthy of your time. Yet a difference of opinion does not deem a conversation useless. A good listener will process the other person's thoughts and try to visualize why they feel the way they do, in a way that is the most beneficial to them. A salesman's best tool is knowing the exact needs of their customer on which they can base their sales pitch.

For example, one of the most common sources of friction between couples relates to personal finances. Your spouse may want a vacation while you want to invest this money into an index fund for retirement. Whilst investing in the future may be the most sensible thing to do financially, listen to the arguments of your spouse to understand why they feel this way. Perhaps they wish to create lifelong memories before starting a family. Perhaps precious memories between the two of you are more important to them than a few thousand dollars down the line. There is no correct answer here. Memories have no monetary value, so you cannot directly compare the two. The value, therefore, comes from opinion alone. From here you may be able to create a compromise that works for both of you because both of your opinions are equally valid if you were to take a step back and realize this. But by arguing, without truly seeking to understand, a productive conclusion will never be found. Effective communication comes not in the form of agreeing with the other person - you may communicate well but never come to the same conclusion (think debates) - but from understanding where the other person is coming from. This open-mindedness may also open your mind to a way of thinking you had perhaps not appreciated before.

More selfishly, listening also greatly benefits you. It often unlocks deeper and more meaningful conversations and extracts knowledge from others that may never have surfaced. Enlightening stories, knowledge, and experiences will be revealed that cannot be gathered from books. Think of people as huge untapped vats of knowledge who will gladly pass it on to those who are willing to listen. I had been working just a few cubicles over from a colleague who I saw every day for over two years. We made idle chit-chat when passing, but I never really got to know him to any significant degree as we were both a little introverted. One day we were assigned to bid on an airport construction project, where we drove an hour out to assess the site. When conversing with him a little deeper on the drive down, we started talking about the housing market, as I was looking to move houses. The more we spoke, the more I asked questions and delved deeper into a more meaningful conversation. Eventually, I made the surprising discovery that he was a serial property developer and owned dozens of houses, apartments, and commercial properties. He was a multi-millionaire and quite probably the wealthiest and most knowledgeable person in our entire company. He then went on to help me buy my first rental property. Although he was a mild fellow, and probably because of it, he was excited for someone to show him so much attention and recognize his success. He was very willing to help me and went far out of his way to get me started in the industry. Had I taken the time to get to know him a little better previously, I could have started years earlier. Had I not been lucky enough to go on that random trip with him, however, I might have never even started at all.

The advice outlined in this chapter will enable you to become a better conversationalist by providing structure to conversation and facilitating a platform for others to share information more readily. By doing so you will make the other person feel valued and rewarded, and will ultimately be rewarded yourself through better relationships and greater opportunities.

Task:

Next time you are in conversation with someone, play a sort of friendly game to see how much information you can encourage the other person to divulge. Instead of making idle chit-chat about what you got up to at the weekend, listen intently to what the other person is saying and try to connect on a more personal level. If someone tells you they went hiking, ask how often they go hiking. You might find out they are passionate hikers and you now have a valuable piece of information about what engages them emotionally. Perhaps you may even get a future invite.

Remember the five key components: Eye contact, body language, avoid interrupting, ask questions, and paraphrase. All five components keep the emphasis on the other person and provide a platform for others to expand their thoughts. It also proves to them that you are attentive and are genuinely interested in what they have to say.

3.5 Remember a Person's Name

I"It was the craziest thing," said John Standing with tears running down his face. "Poor old Peter Roster didn't stand a chance. The second he walked across the road he was hit by a truck who came speeding out of nowhere." Nancy Thornton then rushed out of her house to administer first aid and called for an ambulance. But it was too late.

How many of the three names in the above passage can you remember? Most would not be able to remember all three, especially in scenarios such as the above where there is so much stimulus. Yet the ability to remember someone's name is such a simple but immensely powerful tool that is often wasted. Remember someone's name and you will have paid a tremendous compliment.

We all like to be acknowledged as the unique individuals we are. We like to feel that we matter. That we are significant. This is why many wealthy people spend exorbitant sums to plaster their name around the world. In 2015, David Geffen, an American business magnate, made a $100 million donation to the Lincoln Center in exchange for the renaming of the Avery Fisher Hall to the David Geffen Hall. More recently, billionaire banker Sandy Weill and his wife Joan withdrew a $20 million donation to Paul Smith's College after the school was unable to change its name to Joan Weill-Paul Smith's College.

Using someone's name in conversation helps to break down awkward social barriers. It also makes conversations much more personal and builds an air of confidence and familiarity that will benefit the remaining conversation. It is a tool used by those who wish to build familiarity, especially by cold callers, complaint departments, and helplines. Next time you communicate with a service where you wish to make a complaint, notice how the first thing they do will be to introduce themselves. It is harder to be angry at someone when you know their name and where there is more of a personal connection. The second thing these people will ask is for your name, where they will then repeat it often to further build the appearance of familiarity.

With the social barrier reduced, the regular application of a name establishes stronger social connections. When repeating a name in conversion, it emphasizes to the other person that they are valued enough to have their name remembered. The person knows that they're more than just another face in the crowd and that you care enough to communicate on an individual level. It makes them feel important enough for you to have made the effort and that they made an impression. Remember the name and you will have paid a subtle and very effective compliment. Forget or misspell it, however, and you will most likely cause insult.

This insult is rarely intentional, however. Most are simply too focused on trying to make a good impression themselves as opposed to listening intently to others. Much of our focus is dedicated on how we come across to others, such as ensuring we are smiling, saying the right things and that our body language remains receptive. As a result, we often forget a person's name just a few minutes after it is first mentioned. In some cases, the name never registers at all. Yet if we dedicated just a little attention away from ourselves for just a moment, and directed it towards actively remembering a person's name, we would instantly appear much more confident and approachable without having to focus so directly on making a good impression in the first place.

To ensure you remember a person's name, make sure you catch it as early as possible in the conversation. If they don't introduce themselves, introduce yourself. They will almost always introduce themselves in response. Once you have the name, instantly repeat it out loud to pay an immediate and powerful complement. For example, they may say "Hi, I'm John" and you respond with "Hi John, I'm Mark" or "John, I'm Mark, how's it going?". Repeating the name out loud will help you recall the name later. To cement the name in your immediate memory, I like to repeat the name 5 times internally whilst focusing on their facial appearance to build the connection between face and name.

There are many other tips people use to build these connections. Some use alliteration, such as "big nose Neil" or "Big Ben". I find the simplest and most effective technique, however, is to simply focus intensely on linking the name and face. Repeat the name internally at least 5 times and externally two or three times throughout the brief initial conversation. Over time you will start to perform this process subconsciously and develop what I have found to be the simplest way to become much more personable whilst also paying an immediate compliment.

Task:

Remember this simple process every time you meet someone new or would benefit from remembering a name. Firstly, manually divert attention away from you and towards them. If they do not introduce themselves, introduce yourself. This is almost always reciprocated with them revealing their name.

Respond with a simple line that repeats the name out loud. "Hi John, my name is Mark". This is an easy compliment and immediately shifts the conversation to a more personal one.

Secondly, repeat the name five times in your mind whilst focusing on their facial details to build the visual memory.

Thirdly, try to repeat the name three times in the entire conversation, one at the introduction, one in the middle, and one to say goodbye.

3.6 You are the Average of the People You Spend the Most Time With.

Why is someone born in Tennessee almost five times more likely to end up in prison than someone born in Massachusetts? Why does the average worker in San Jose earn almost $34,000 more than someone in Tennessee? And why do Black or African American men earn $0.87 for every dollar a White man earns? The sad fact is that humans are a product of not just their nature but also their nurture. The environment we grow up in largely affects who we become and ultimately influences our future quality of life.

While much of this unbalance is impossible to avoid during our early years, as independent decision-making adults we can alter our current environment to address the balance. Many young adults, having graduated college, face the difficult decision of either moving back to their home state or branching out on their own to some of the major hubs in search of better opportunities. Actors travel to LA where the entertainment industry dominates. Programmers flock to Silicon Valley where tech titans flourish while writers and editors cluster around New York to mingle with top-tier journalists.

Geography itself is not the direct cause of differing opportunities, rather it is the people who tend to congregate within these areas. Ultimately it is the interaction, and ability to learn from, these top-tier industry leaders that provide the greatest opportunities. Jim Rohn first coined the prose that "you're the average of the five people you spend the most time with". You will therefore become a more capable software engineer the more time you spend with top-tier software engineers, many of which reside in Silicon Valley. According to research by social psychologist Dr. David McClelland of Harvard University, the people you habitually associate with determines as much as 95 percent of your success or failure in life. For many this can be negative; a major reason for above-average Black incarceration rates is because a higher percentage of Blacks grow up in poorer areas where crime rates are higher. Yet for others this can be beneficial; students who study at Ivy League Universities have access to better professional networks after graduating.

Whilst hyperbolic, Jim Rohn's statement is not limited to just five people. In fact, the effect is far wider-reaching and can include almost anyone you have, or have not, ever met.

The first major study on the breadth of social influence was conducted by Nicholas Christakis and James Fowler of Harvard University. The original intent of the study was to assess how social networks might affect heart health. The pair examined the data set from the Framingham Heart Study, one of the largest and longest-running health studies ever concluded, when they realized the data revealed that it was more than just heart health that was affected by social networks.

The pair analyzed the data to see what the effects of family members and friends were on something fairly simple and objective: obesity. According to their results, if a friend of yours becomes obese, you are 45 percent more likely to gain weight over the next four years. More surprisingly, however, was the finding that if a friend of your friend becomes obese, your likelihood of gaining weight increases by about 20 percent — even if you have never met that particular person (presumably because your friend is more likely to be influenced by their friend, which in turn makes it more likely for you to be affected by your friend). The effect continues to spread even further from this initial relationship. If a friend of a friend of your friend develops obesity, you are still 10 percent more likely to gain weight over chance statistics. Even if you do not know these distant friends, the statistics show that these trends from people within your realm of contacts do have an indirect effect on you.

This same phenomenon was also observed with smokers. The study found that if your friend smokes, you are 61 percent more likely to smoke yourself. If a friend of your friend smokes, you are 29 percent more likely to smoke. And for a friend of a friend of your friend, the likelihood is 11 percent. These trends confirm something that has always been implied but never statistically determined; the network and community you spend time with directly influence your character and mindset.

When considering your immediate social network, the three areas the majority tend to spend the most time with is family, friends, and colleagues. Family is the most influential; smokers are most likely to have smoking parents and degree earners are most likely to come from families whose parents also have a degree. We cannot control our family, however, and many remain loyal to long term friends despite their poor influences. Similarly, we are often stuck with the people we work with, for better or worse. We cannot simply drop them from our lives, but we can limit their influence on us if necessary, by limiting exposure time with them or through mindfulness and being aware when negativity or poor habits start to encroach in our circle of influence.

Ultimately you will become the equilibrium of all the people who influence you in any way, no matter how small. Much like how hot water mixed with cold water will find a temperature in the middle, you too will find yourself in the equilibrium of the people around you. You can think of this average as numerical. To find your average, simply rate the people you spend the most time with out of 10, with 10 being the best influence and 1 the poorest. For example, my cousin has always settled for the easiest path in life. In contrast with me, who always sought adventure, he wanted a comfortable and simple life. Whilst not necessarily a negative, this sort of life is not for me. So, when I first excitedly told him of my dream to work abroad, he immediately scoffed his nose. "Why would you want to travel to a new country, with no friends, no job, and no house?" This hit me hard and almost led me to miss the best experience of my life. As much as I respect my cousin, I rate him a 4 out of 10 in terms of his influence on me, at least in terms of adventure. Note, however, that this rating is relative; whilst he rates a four for me, he may rate a nine to someone else with similar goals. One of my best friends from university, however, has always had an admirable entrepreneurial spirit and went on to start a very successful digital advertising company. We converse regularly and he always makes me strive to better myself. I rate his influence an eight. The average of just these two people blends my social network to a 6 out of 10 in terms of positive influence on me.

If I want to increase this average number, as we should all strive to do, I have two options. I either need to reduce the amount of time I spend with lower numbers or increase the time I spend with higher numbers (or ideally both). I enjoy the time I spend with my cousin, despite our different ambitions, so I would seek to further my social network of people who are more positively aligned with my specific goals. If I wanted to improve my property portfolio, I would seek out some networking events where these people gather. I might now spend time with three new people who I rate a 9 out of 10 in terms of helping to get me where I want to be. My new average would now be 7.8 out of 10. I am now more likely to advance my property career through associating with higher quality people.

If someone is bringing down your average, you may need to address the amount of time you spend with them to reduce their influence on you. You should also continuously strive to raise your average by seeking higher quality people relative to your goals. Giving a silent critique of the people you most often associate with may sound judgmental and downright ruthless; but understanding their influence on your performance is critical to future success. Remember, this number is not an indication of them as a person, it is merely in terms relative to your specific goals. You can spend significant time with Gandhi but in terms of your football career, he will still rate a 1 out of 10 in terms of influence.

Now you can't simply drop your family and eliminate them from your life, but you can cut down the amount of time or influence they exert on you. At the very least, you can be more aware of the detrimental effect they may have on you. But you absolutely can control the quality of new people you introduce into your immediate social network. Looking to get into better shape this year? Hang out in areas where healthy people tend to gather such as sports clubs and gyms. Want to get into real estate? Attend night classes or search online forums for other enthusiasts. Simply mingling with people who are already where you want to be in life significantly increases your chances of reaching these levels.

Many entrepreneurs strive to be the smartest person in the room on every issue. But if you're always the smartest person, you're hurting yourself. You want to surround yourself with people who can run circles around you in as many areas as possible, people who are exponentially better in a variety of ways. As a business owner, you need to employ people who are more knowledgeable than you, at least in the area for which you are employing them. Always seek to mingle with people you deem more successful than you and where you ultimately want to be in life. It is the only way to continually raise your average.

Task:

Assess the five to ten people you spend the most time with. In terms of your goals and aspirations, rate them out of ten as to how good an influence they are on you. Average the total to ascertain the influence of your immediate social network on your life. If you feel life is stagnant, this may be a significant contributing factor.

One should continuously seek to increase this average by reducing time spent with low scorers and increase time spent with higher scorers. Brainstorm how you might be able to start networking and expanding your social network. Joining clubs, courses, or networking sessions are just a few ways to mingle with more influential people.

Don't strive to be the best in the room. If you are, you have outgrown this space and are likely to stagnate. Seek a greater quality of people and therefore better opportunities.

3.7 Learn the Art of Body Language

Body Language, the process of communicating nonverbally through conscious or unconscious gestures and movements, forms a significant part of daily social interactions. From facial expressions to body movements, sometimes the most powerful way to make a statement comes not from the mouth but from the projection of the subconscious through movements of the body.

It has been estimated that body language accounts for between 60-65 percent of total communication. It is a tool that humans, and animals, have used to communicate since time immemorial when speech was not as sophisticated as it is today. Yet despite our complex languages, humans are still subject to primal habits, and body language still proves to be a very effective tool for interpreting the intentions of others as well as projecting our own subtle thoughts.

The importance of landing a good first impression is clear to all, whether we are the ones judging or being judged. First impressions are extremely influential and difficult to reverse. Connoting confidence within the first few seconds of a conversation through the appropriate use of body language can provide a subtle edge that helps align a person's mind with yours; we are much more agreeable with people who exude confidence and trust. Studies have found that nonverbal cues have over four times the impact on the impression you make than spoken words, so understanding and utilizing social cues to your advantage can open doors.

Some people are inherently better at reading and projecting body language than others. Like any other skill, however, it can be learned, and only knowledge, time, and experience will improve your competence.

You need only look at politicians to witness this skill in action. Body language is a staple of the fundamental training curriculum for politicians. Whilst some, such as Mitt Romney and Bill Clinton, have become very adept at this art, others, such as Donald Trump, show a distinct lack of ability. A quick google search will yield hundreds of results detailing Donald Trump's most awkward body language blunders. It's clear that while he is being coached, Trump is not enough of a practiced politician to keep the rouse up all the time, which is not surprising considering his lack of political experience compared to other seasoned veterans. Politicians build this skill over a whole career.

Key fundamentals of body language consist of three main areas: facial expressions, body proxemics, and externals. The first, facial expressions, are the most immediately noticeable as emotions are almost always first expressed through micro-expressions in the face, occurring as quickly as 0.04 - 0.07 of a second. You can tell a genuine happy facial expression from a "fake" happy one by looking to see how much of the muscles at the side of the eyes are engaged. A genuine smile engages these muscles and is immediately noticeable to those who specifically look for it. Google pictures to observe for yourself. Eye contact is also very telling of a person's mental state. Those who constantly divert their gaze come across as uncomfortable. Those who can hold their gaze appear more attentive to the conversation and more confident in their communications. Too much, however, can make both parties uncomfortable.

Body Proxemics defines how we move within our immediate space. Typical "alphas", those extroverts who exude confidence, will own their immediate and surrounding space confidently. Confident people take up space and relax; they try to look as large and open as possible. Insecure people, on the other hand, are constricted and taut. When uncomfortable or anxious they tend to curl up into as little space as possible in the hope of finding some security in their smaller comfort zones.

How you present your body also reveals a lot. Standing square with someone, i.e. torso to torso, conveys more confidence and attention than when your torso is aimed slightly away. We are all guilty of starting to turn away from someone when we wish to leave a conversation, such as when we do not have time to engage or when we are uncomfortable with the topic of discussion. A person standing closer, or faced directly toward you, shows interest in the interaction (or possibly even you!). Men and women tend to behave slightly differently here, however. When males communicate, they tend to stand at right angles to each other, not face to face. Face-to-face is confrontational, but shoulder-to-shoulder in an "L" shape is much more comfortable for men. Women prefer face-to-face, however. Pay attention to these habits next time you are in the office.

Foot positioning can also divulge subtle information. People will almost always orientate their feet in the direction they want to move. So next time you notice someone pointing their feet in a slightly different direction to their torso, take this as a hint that they might be wanting to move somewhere else.

Mimicking body movements is also a great indicator of influence. If you're having a conversation with someone and they start to copy your body language, whether it be scratching your face, crossing your arms, or putting your hands in your pockets, it means they are responding positively to you.

Mirroring body language is a primal mechanism for social bonding. The most obvious forms of mirroring are yawning and smiling. When next communicating, pay attention to when someone else starts to smile. You will almost always instantly start smiling back, regardless of how interested you may or may not be in the conversation. Some scientists have concluded that only sociopaths are immune to contagious yawning. Mirroring body language is a non-verbal way to say 'I am like you; I feel the same'. You can check this habit by intentionally changing your position to see if they do too. This also works in reverse; you can get people to like you more by copying their body language and verbal cues. This can be very helpful in interviews, but ensure it remains subtle.

Lastly, we have external indicators. Clothes, jewelry, sunglasses, and hair are all extensions of our body language. Not only do certain colors and styles send signals to others, how we interact with these items is also telling. Do they constantly self-preen or touch their hair? Do they keep fidgeting with their watch or jewelry? These may be subconscious cues to create a distraction when confronted with a lack of confidence or a feeling of discomfort.

Group social dynamics can also provide mountains of information. To see who the alpha or natural leader is in a group, look to see who people immediately look to when laughing. People will often look to who they subconsciously perceive to be the alpha, as a sort of social validation of how they should be acting. If the leader laughs, it is ok for them to also laugh. If they don't laugh, then others are also less likely to laugh. Don't believe me? When someone next makes a joke in a group setting, look to see where others avert their attention. Odds are they will look at who they perceive as their leader, such as managers or bosses. Incidentally, if someone is interested in you romantically, they will tend to look at you if they see or hear something funny, as a primal validation from you. You have to gauge the context, but the general rule is that people tend to look to those they respect as social validation, usually because they exert the most influence on that particular person. This won't apply to everyone, one's leader may not necessarily be someone else's (people may have different bosses, for example).

Recognizing and interpreting the body language of others, known as decoding, is only the first part of becoming adept at reading body language. The second part is encoding, where you apply these skills to communicate your own wants and needs more efficiently. This could be when negotiating a big sale, asking someone on a first date, or even negotiating for your life, as most special ops military units are trained to do.

These few insights barely scratch the surface of the art of body language. I would suggest further reading if it interests you. It must also be noted that body language is far from an exact science; interpretations vary wildly between person to person. But in general, we can find trends, such as those mentioned above, which allow us to gather more information about what others may be thinking to facilitate better communication. With this knowledge at the tip of your fingers, your conversations will gradually become more meaningful and pave the way for greater opportunities.

4. Health

Health advice may seem out of place in a self-help book, but to become the best version of ourselves we have to ensure our body remains as sharp as our minds. The body and mind work synergistically; when one suffers so does the other. The body can be thought of as a racecar and your mind its driver. Your mind may be the equivalent of 7-time Championship winner Michael Schumacher, but your progress will also be limited if your vehicle keeps breaking down. Similarly, you may have the best race car in the field but if the driver does not know how to operate it you won't be going anywhere fast. Only when the car and driver are at their peak will you be winning races. The chapters below outline some of the fundamental health acts that should be utilized to ensure our bodies operate at their peak. They provide the strong foundations upon which we can expand.

4.1 Exercise

Exercise. The task we all dread but know needs to be done. Health professionals the world over have been preaching the need for regular exercise for decades, and there is no disputing the health benefits for those who regularly commit to it and the detrimental effects for those who do not. What is perhaps not as common knowledge, however, is just how far-reaching these health benefits can be. Not only does exercise improve your immediate sense of wellness but it can also add years onto your lifespan. More importantly, the quality of those years will be significantly improved, allowing you to stay mobile further into old age. The aim of this chapter is not to tell you to exercise regularly, you already know this, and I do not wish to patronize but to energize your motivation after identifying just how far a small commitment every day can go towards improving your life.

Firstly, exercise fortifies your entire body. This includes not only muscles but also organs, arguably more important. The heart, for example, an organ largely made up of a type of muscle tissue called cardiac muscle, operates more efficiently when exercised regularly. As you exercise, your muscles consume up to three times as much oxygen as when they are resting, and your heart rate increases to cope with the increased demand. The more you exercise, the more efficient the heart becomes at managing this demand, and the less likely you are to succumb to fatigue.

Heart disease is a silent killer and the number one cause of death in the United States. Regular exercise increases the blood carrying capacity of the left ventricle, making it easier for the heart to pump oxygenated blood to all organs, muscles, and systems of the body. More blood means more cell repairs, helping you recover better from injury and even staving off the diminishing effects of age, ensuring you look and feel younger. Apart from the obvious cardiovascular benefits, positive physiological changes are also promoted through regular exercise, such as encouraging the heart's arteries to dilate more readily, which allows blood to circulate more freely. The sympathetic nervous system (which controls heart rate and blood pressure) will also be able to moderate itself more efficiently. Although the benefits of regular exercise are often long term, the body is so quick to adapt that improvements can be noticed almost immediately after exercising.

Another incredible effect of exercise on the heart lies in a biological mechanism called ischemic preconditioning (IPC). A heart attack occurs when one or more of your coronary arteries become blocked. "The idea is that when you have a coronary blockage and you exercise, the area of heart beyond the blockage is starved for blood supply — more so than when you're at rest," says cardiologist Dr. Meagan Wasfy of the Cardiovascular Performance Program at Harvard-affiliated Massachusetts General Hospital. "That sets up a number of molecular and metabolic pathways that help the heart adapt to that inadequate blood flow," she explains. Although IPC does not prevent blockages of arteries in the first place, it significantly improves the chances of survival for those who have them. Animal studies suggest that ischemic preconditioning seems to protect the heart if a heart attack does occur later on by as much as 50 percent, with this protective effect lasting up to 48 hours immediately after exercising. Even for a slim and relatively in-shape person, you never truly know how far you are from a heart attack. For those who are older, perhaps not in as great health, or have a family background of heart attacks, regular exercise can significantly reduce the damage if a heart attack were to occur through ischemic preconditioning.

There is a myriad of other benefits of regular exercise. In a study of more than 14,800 women, those who had the highest levels of aerobic fitness were 55 percent less likely to die from breast cancer than those who were sedentary. Women considered moderately fit had a 33 percent lower risk of developing the disease. Colon cancer is one of the most extensively studied cancers concerning physical activity.

A 2009 meta-analysis of 52 epidemiologic studies that examined the association between physical activity and colon cancer risk found that the most physically active individuals had a 24 percent lower risk of colon cancer than those who were the least physically active. The mechanism behind this relates to the reduction of growth factors and hormones, such as insulin and estrogen. Regular exercise can also reduce the amount of time it takes for food to travel through the digestive system, which decreases gastrointestinal tract exposure to possible carcinogens.

Just 30 minutes a day can keep obesity away. The worldwide prevalence of obesity nearly tripled between 1975 and 2016, with an estimated 30 percent of the global population now considered obese. It is a problem that burdens not only individuals but also state funds; the United States devotes over 20 percent of their annual medical spending to combat the effects of obesity. Exercise can help to prevent harmful effects associated with obesity, particularly the development of insulin resistance (failure of the body's cells to respond to insulin). It also reduces inflammation by providing greater quantities of oxygenated and nutrient-rich blood to all areas of the body, therefore improving joint mobility. The immune system is strengthened through boosting levels of immunoglobulins, proteins that bolster the immune system and ward off infection. "Every sweat session you do can help strengthen your immune function for about 24 hours," says Cedric Bryant, Ph.D., chief science officer for the American Council on Exercise. Amid a global coronavirus pandemic, with people around the world dying in the thousands, there has never been a better time to have a strengthened immune system.

Regular exercise can provide better functioning telomeres (the DNA that bookends our chromosomes and protects them from damage), which studies show can slow the aging process. Yes, regular exercise really does keep you looking younger. Research at the Cooper Clinic in Dallas found that as little as 30 minutes of cardio, from walking to rowing, three to five days a week can add six years to the average lifespan. That may be the difference between meeting a grandchild and not. Regular resistance training focusing more on muscle strength also combats feebleness and poor posture in old age.

Perhaps the most underappreciated aspect of exercise, however, is the strengthening of the mind. Humans are estimated to only use around 40 percent of their potential capacity when they feel they "hit the wall". The mind, in a bid to protect the body from harm, acts as a physical limiter to uncomfortable situations. This applies not only to physical feats, such as endurance running but also to mental feats, such as persevering with a business that has hit hard times. Exercise is an easily accessible technique to allow you to push past this 40 percent barrier, and therefore strengthen your mental fortitude.

Apologies if the above feels repetitive and tedious, but the benefits are so vast they are worth expanding upon. Even if one does not fear the consequences of poor health, they might at least appreciate the myriad benefits that it presents. The question remains what sort of exercise one should perform and how often? There is no single correct answer here, but the consensus amongst experts suggests at least 150 minutes of moderate aerobic activity or 75 minutes of vigorous aerobic activity a week (or a combination of both). This works out as 20 minutes of moderate activity a day for seven days a week or 30 minutes for five days (half for vigorous activity). If this sounds daunting for you, build up to it; any amount of exercise is better than none at all and some of the effects are immediate. But these limits should be the ultimate aim.

The Department of Health and Human Services also recommends strength training exercises for all major muscle groups at least twice a week. Aim to do sets of exercises using a weight or resistance level heavy enough to tire your muscles after 10 to 15 repetitions. Alternatively, exercise classes such as yoga or boxing will provide the same benefit with an added social component. I have gotten into the habit of performing 20 minutes of cardio every morning after waking up. Any time is acceptable, however, at long as it is unavoidable and consistent. Whilst all forms of exercise are good for the heart, low impact exercises are better for long term health, especially for those who take heed of this advice early in life and commit to it for the next, 40, 50, or 60 years. Running is a higher impact exercise and therefore takes a slightly greater toll on joints and delicate cartilage in the knees. I use an elliptical machine which is low impact and works the whole body, but rowing, cycling, and swimming are all excellent alternatives. Still, a jog around the block every morning is certainly better than nothing.

A common mistake many make when exercising is not exercising hard enough. Whilst you certainly don't have to set any records or work to exhaustion every workout, you need to raise your heart's BPM (beats per minute) to a high enough level to elicit any meaningful benefits. It is recommended that you exercise within 55 to 85 percent of your maximum heart rate for at least 20 to 30 minutes to get the best results from aerobic exercise. Optimum and maximum rates per age group that you should be targeting can be found online. Most gym equipment these days have heart sensors built-in. Smartwatches such as Apple watches and Fitbits are also a great way to ensure your BPM remains in these ranges.

Although seemingly unfitting in a self-improvement book, the significance of a healthy body cannot be underestimated in maintaining a healthy mindset. Furthermore, these short time commitments of just 30 minutes a day can be crafted into a habit that becomes automatic over time. Instead of getting home and watching TV on the couch for 30 minutes, purchase a cheap exercise bike and watch it from there. Your mind and body are synergistic - when one suffers so too does the other. For example, when mentally stressed the body tends to lose weight. When the body is physically stressed, the efficiency and capability of the mind reduce in turn.

4.2 Massage Therapy

If only the body came with a maintenance manual like any other hard-working piece of machinery. Unfortunately, it doesn't and we often pay the price. We service our vehicles every few thousand miles with new oil and parts to ensure optimal running conditions and avoid unscheduled break downs. Yet we do not take the same approach with our bodies, a much more valuable asset which works longer and harder than most non-organic machines ever do.

There are around 600 muscles in the body that work together to create a highly capable musculoskeletal system; just a simple smile requires 10 muscles to fire together. Like anything that is worked regularly, parts wear and need maintenance, and the more these parts are worked the more frequent this maintenance needs to occur. This is yet another lesson I learned the hard way, having regularly strength trained in my younger years (and to a lesser degree still today). I would go to the gym almost daily and lift as heavy a weight as was physically possible, week after week, and year after year. Although the body is remarkably good at rebuilding and repairing muscles, sustained heavy use eventually takes its toll on the muscle fibers and surrounding fascia which haven't evolved to take such a prolonged pounding. As such they often cannot be maintained by the body alone.

Excessive use of these muscles (which includes standing or sitting for long periods of time), fatigues, and damages the muscle fibers. This is the whole premise of bodybuilding, where the damaged muscles repair bigger and stronger as the body adapts to the increased physical demands. Excessive amounts of damage, however, results in a toughening of the smaller muscle fiber sarcomeres and fascia (a band or sheet of connective tissue, primarily collagen, beneath the skin that attaches, stabilizes, encloses, and separates muscles and other internal organs). This results in what we often refer to as muscle "knots" (more accurately known as myofascial trigger points), which appear as small bump-like areas of muscle that can be painful to the touch, affecting up to 85 percent of the population. If you haven't performed any mechanical maintenance of your muscles recently, such as massage therapy, chances are you have muscle knots to some degree which will be affecting your general health, perhaps without you even realizing.

Found typically in the back, shoulders, and neck, muscle "knots" are stiff bands of muscle that have a hard knob in the center. The pain can either pop up spontaneously (active) or when the trigger point is pressed (latent). But in all cases, muscle knots cause pain to radiate beyond the trigger point into the surrounding muscles. Trigger points are complex and have a variety of possible causes. There is a lot more research to be conducted on the matter, but the best available evidence suggests that muscle knots are the result of overuse, such as heavy lifting or repetitive activities. Other causes may include psychological stress, poor ergonomics, bad posture (especially sitting for long periods of time), fatigue, dehydration, unhealthy eating habits, sleep disturbances, and joint problems. If any of these sound familiar, tight fascia and muscles may well be affecting your general health.

Muscle fibers contract and relax in order to lengthen and shorten. However, when we sit at a desk for prolonged periods of time, with very little movement, these muscle fibers begin to stick to each other, forming a knot. Bad posture, such as hunching and rounding the shoulders, also puts stress on muscles, and after enough time the stress will cause the formation of scar tissue. Depending on where in the body the muscle knot is located, it may cause seemingly unrelated pain in other areas. For example, a muscle knot in the neck can send pain into the base of the skull, causing a tension headache. If you suffer from phantom headaches, unsuspecting muscle knots in the neck is a common cause. There are very few people who get through life without ever experiencing a muscle knot. 97 percent of people with chronic pain have trigger points, and almost 100 percent of people with neck pain have them. Chances are strong that you too have knots if you rarely receive any form of massage, even if you don't yet feel the effects of them.

To counter these detrimental effects, and keep the body regularly maintained and serviced, massage therapy should be regularly incorporated into your schedule. Think of it as a service for your body similar to how you would service your vehicle every few thousand miles. The benefits of massage therapy are numerous. When the body is tense and under stress, it produces unhealthy levels of cortisol (the stress hormone) which can contribute to weight gain, sleeplessness, digestive problems, and headaches, which can all develop into more serious problems. Massage therapy has been shown to decrease cortisol levels, allowing the body to enter a recovery mode. Massage therapy also triggers lasting feelings of relaxation and improved mood.

Massage also promotes the circulation of blood to the affected muscles where nutrient-rich and oxygenated blood can deliver all the nutrients these muscles so desperately require. In turn, this reduces stiffness and edema (swelling) in the muscles and joints whilst also increasing mobility, ensuring you move more freely and with less pain. Actively Improving your circulation through massage therapy also makes it easier for the body to take care of itself. Like how a blockage in a car cooling system needs manually removing, once removed the coolant will flow by itself and you no longer need to worry about overheating. Once you manually remove the blockage in your muscles, blood flows freely and the body can then heal itself more efficiently.

Whilst the body is a master healer, able to overcome incredible damage to both muscles and organs, it cannot rid the body of muscle knots. The toughened fibers are simply too tough. Instead, they must be released manually with pressure (often quite painfully). Whilst the science behind massage therapy is not definitively known, it is thought that knots are long-term cramping of the muscle, which the body creates in an effort to adapt to heavy and repetitive weight. It is a defense mechanism to avoid further damage to muscle fibers by clotting together for greater resistance. Whilst it may protect the muscle short term, it negatively affects other areas such as joints and ligaments longer term. Physical manipulation of the cramped area is the only way to effectively loosen these toughened fibers, and as a result, knowledgeable masseuses are worth their weight in gold.

Unfortunately, massage therapists are usually relatively costly. Expect to pay upwards of $100 an hour and even more for more established therapists. Yet an hour a week, or even a month is a great investment in your long-term health, and a small price to pay for continued health. After just a few sessions, I guarantee you will feel the benefits. Getting a massage used to be a luxury but as increasing numbers realize the benefit it provides, they've been growing in demand and popularity. Now that massage therapy is considered a mainstream treatment option, many insurance companies provide coverage for treatment sessions. Check with your benefits package to see if you are entitled. If the price is still too steep, research online how to perform basic massage maintenance on yourself. 20 minutes of self-massage is now a daily habit for me, meaning I only need to see a professional every couple of weeks. A lot of trigger points can be targeted yourself once you know what you are doing with simple tools such as a foam roller and a lacrosse ball.

Left untended, the body will eventually tighten up and restrict motion significantly, especially when approaching old age. Those unfortunate seniors often sighted with limited motion and hunched backs are most likely the result of decades of poor posture and poor muscle maintenance. With the modern curse of sitting in front of a desk for hours on end, poor mobility in old age will become a greater issue as this newer generation of workers grows old. You owe it to your family, and yourself, to ensure you avoid this plight. If you don't look after your body, you can't expect it to look after you.

4.3 Eat Enough Good Foods

Another obvious and uninsightful tip. But this generic topic has a twist. Whilst most advice focuses on avoiding bad foods, I intentionally emphasize the need to eat enough good foods, which studies have found to be more important. Obviously, the healthiest results derive from both eliminating poor foods and introducing more nutritious foods, but be mindful of the fact that a poor diet is not defined merely by bad quality foods, but also the lack of good quality foods.

A poor diet is even more damaging to health than you might think. Globally, one in five deaths is associated with a poor diet, equating to 11 million self-inflicted deaths annually. According to the Global Burden of Disease Study, which tracks trends in consumption of

15 dietary factors from 1990 to 2017 throughout 195 countries, a greater proportion of deaths were attributed to insufficient quantities of foods such as whole grains, fruits, nuts and seeds than by diets with high levels of foods like trans fats, sugary drinks, and high levels of red and processed meats. In essence, more deaths were related to a lack of nutrient-rich foods than that of unhealthy foods. Diets high in sodium, low in whole grains, and low in fruit together accounted for more than half of all diet-related global deaths in 2017.

The largest shortfalls in optimal intake were seen for nuts, seeds, milk, and whole grains. The largest excesses were seen for sugar-sweetened beverages, processed meats, and sodium. On average, the world ate just 12 percent of the recommended amount of nuts and seeds (around 3g average intake per day, compared with 21g recommended), and drank around ten times the recommended amount of sugar-sweetened beverages (49g average intake, compared with 3g recommended). In addition, the global diet included 16 percent of the recommended amount of milk (71g average intake per day, compared with 435g recommended), about a quarter of the recommended amount of whole grains (29g average intake per day, compared with 125g recommended).

So, one of the best changes you can instantly make to your diet is to simply add 21g of nuts to your diet (a small snack pot) and a large bowl of oatmeal everyday (for increased whole grains and milk). These two simple additions will overcome the two largest sources of dietary deficiencies shown in the study.

The human body truly is a marvel in biological and chemical

engineering, having been the benefactor of over 200,000 years of evolution. It is a highly efficient manufacturer of skin, muscle, and bone, and produces millions of red blood cells every day which carry nutrients and oxygen to every outpost of the body. All these highly complex processes are automatically controlled by a series of complex networks sending nerve signals along thousands of miles of neurological pathways. In order to sustain all of these complex mechanisms, your body requires sufficient quantities of raw materials. These include at least 30 various vitamins, minerals, and dietary components that your body needs but cannot manufacture on its own in sufficient amounts. Among the most common are Vitamin D, folic acid, zinc, and iron.

Vitamins and minerals are often called micronutrients because your body requires only small quantities of them. Yet failing to get even these small quantities virtually guarantees disease. A lack of Vitamin C, for example, has long been known to cause scurvy, characterized by swollen and bleeding gums and the opening of previously healed wounds, which particularly affected poorly nourished sailors until the end of the 18th century. A deficiency in Vitamin D, common in people who are infrequently exposed to direct sunlight, can cause rickets, a condition marked by soft, weak bones that can lead to skeletal deformities such as bowed legs. To help combat diseases such as rickets, the U.S. has fortified milk with vitamin D since the 1930s.

It can be overwhelming to try and analyze every vitamin and mineral the body needs and in what quantities. In fact, for the average person, it would be essentially impossible. There are over 30 different vitamins and minerals, each responsible for their own unique task in maintaining the human body and each with various specific health issues related when deficient, some much more potent than others.

There is one simple strategy to ensure we consume sufficient quantities of each required vitamin and mineral to remain healthy, however; and that is to simply eat a broad variety of foods. In a modern world of packaged meals and fast food, it can be easy to eat the same meals over and over again. The overwhelming amounts of sugar, salt, and chemicals, although damaging, are not the worst part of these foods, rather it is the lack of vital vitamins and minerals the body requires. Even eating salads for every meal, whilst appearing healthy on the surface, will not provide sufficient quantities of vitamins such as B12 and minerals like iron. Whilst salads are a healthy meal, they alone are not a healthy diet as they cannot provide all the micronutrients the body needs. A varied diet, including beans, nuts, meat, milk, whole grains, fruits, and vegetables is by far the best way to a healthy and balanced diet (in appropriate quantities of course). Fad diets, such as Atkins, keto, and even veganism are usually not as healthy long term as regular balanced diets due to a lack of sufficient micronutrients these narrow diets tend to provide.

If you are struggling to gain control over your diet, or simply do not have time to prepare nutritional foods, then remember that if you can only make one change to your diet, ensure it is to introduce more broad and nutritionally varied foods. Fish, leafy greens, nuts, whole grains, and yogurt, in reasonable quantities, are all nutrient-dense superfoods that provide the best bang for your buck. There are numerous studies cited by respected and credible institutions both for and against eating meat, with some stating too much red meat can potentially create cancer-causing compounds when cooked. Yet the body requires vitamins and minerals, such as B12 and heme iron, which are only found in useful quantities in animal-based foods. I'm sure a study could be found both in favor and against almost every food and diet. These are almost all misleading and unhelpful. Just two pragmatic rules will ensure your diet remains healthy. First, eat a wide variety of foods to ensure no deficiencies or overabundance (both dangerous) of any micronutrients. Second, eat all foods in sensible proportions by sticking to recommended daily allowances suggested by respected health institutions. Chances are if you are following the first point you will also be meeting the second point. The takeaway here is that you shouldn't think of a healthy diet purely in terms of removing foods. It is often just as important, if not more, to ensure you provide your body with sufficient quantities of all the nutrients it needs to prosper.

4.4 Mental Health

Health extends far beyond the physical. In fact, according to Roger Williams University, there are five "dimensions of wellness": physical, emotional, social, spiritual, and intellectual. We have already explored the importance of physical wellness and simple steps that can be taken to improve it, but mental health is just as important, yet often undervalued.

Stress and anxiety are inevitable parts of life that affect almost everyone. Seven out of ten adults in the United States say they experience stress or anxiety daily, and most say it interferes at least moderately with their lives, according to the most recent ADAA survey on stress and anxiety disorders. When the American Psychological Association surveyed people in 2008, more people reported physical and emotional symptoms due to stress than they did in 2007, with nearly half reporting an increase in stress over just one year, most likely a result of financial troubles derived from the Great Recession.

Death, divorce, and financial hardship are three of the most common sources of stress which affect people in different ways. Some are more prone to stress and are not as emotionally capable of dealing with it. To those who may currently be stressed or undergoing some form of mental anxiety right now, I cannot pretend to understand what you are going through or tell you how to escape it. Stress is impossible to eliminate, but you can learn to manage it and mitigate its debilitating effects as best you can.

Numerous studies have proven exercise efficient at reducing stress and anxiety levels. According to a recent ADAA online poll, some 14 percent of people make use of regular exercise to cope with tough times. The mental benefits of aerobic exercise have a neurochemical basis - exercise reduces levels of the body's stress hormones, such as adrenaline and cortisol. It also stimulates the production of endorphins, chemicals in the brain that act as the body's natural painkillers, and mood elevators. Endorphins are responsible for the "runner's high" and for feelings of relaxation and optimism that accompany many hard workouts. Regular exercise is a great tool to reduce hindering chemicals responsible for stress levels and instead promoting those responsible for relaxation and pleasure.

We have already seen the importance of a varied and balanced diet on physical health so it should come as no surprise that it is just as vital for mental health. Your brain needs a mix of nutrients in order to stay healthy and function well, just like the other organs in your body. When deficient it cannot fully operate and its health will suffer as a consequence. Vitamin D has been observed to play an important role in mood regulation, as well as nerve and brain health. Similarly, vitamin B12 has been found to help regulate sleep patterns. A varied and balanced diet ensures all the 30-odd vitamins and minerals the body needs to function are available in sufficient amounts. Any deficiencies are almost certain to lead to some form of symptom, mental or physical.

Social interaction is also vital for a healthy mental state. The human brain, and particularly the neocortex (which constitutes its outermost layer), is much larger in humans compared to other primates and mammals of similar size. This is particularly interesting because the neocortex comprises many of the areas within the brain that are concerned with higher social cognition, such as conscious thought, language, behavioral and emotion regulation, as well as empathy. It offers the unique ability to understand the feelings and intentions of others. We are, so to speak, biologically hard-wired to interact with others, and are thus said to be endowed with a "social brain."

These developments are likely the result of simple survival tactics. Social clans of animals provide better protection from predators (through strength in numbers) and ultimately better survival odds. A lack of social interaction, therefore, sends chemical messages to the brain indicating that it may be in danger from predators through isolation. These chemical messages flood the brain with negative emotions, thereby encouraging it to seek social interaction and therefore providing this safety through numbers. Most of the physical threats man once faced from predators no longer exist, but human biology has not yet adapted. We are therefore still subject to our ancient biological needs for social interaction. Unfortunately, simply knowing this does not change anything; we cannot wish away our chemical and neural interactions. We therefore have to fulfill these primal urges for social interaction or fall victim to the flood of chemicals that are designed to cause stress and anxiety.

How one seeks this social interaction will be specific to them. Many people turn to friends and family, but others are not so fortunate. There are a myriad of ways and means of meeting people these days. Online dating and apps can help to meet a romantic partner and there are even similar sites to find friends. Hobby and enthusiast groups are excellent ways to meet like-minded people. Perhaps the best way, in my experience, are exercise groups such as cycling clubs or classes held in most gyms, as everyone is there with the common goal of getting fit, coincidentally another stress buster. For those without an immediate friendship group, this will require an active effort to put yourself out there and try something new, an uncomfortable proposition for many. But it is vital to create these social groups in order to avoid the biological effects on the brain that social isolation induces.

Mindfulness, as touted throughout this book, can help stem the flow of negative emotions when we succumb to periods of poor mental health. We have seen throughout this book that almost all negative thoughts and feelings stem from the limbic system (the chimp), whose split-second reactive thoughts are often harmful and cannot be eliminated. Yet simply being mindful of this fact can help reign in these thoughts and prevent them from escalating. It can be compared to doing poorly on an exam or making a mistake at work. It is easy to turn these events into big deals, such as worrying if you will flunk school or lose your job. The negativity-bias means humans are prone to expecting the worst-case scenario when, more often than not, it turns out to be relatively harmless. This is hard to control without the power of hindsight and is even more difficult the younger and less experienced with your emotions you are. It is not something that can be actively changed either; only through time and experience will you start to recognize the true context of negative events. But simply being mindful can help to reason your thoughts and rationalize them within their context. Athletes are excellent practitioners of mindfulness, for example. Through years of experience, athletes can push through immense levels of pain and fatigue as they know pain is short term and are more mindful of the context of their position. An untrained person, even of equivalent fitness, would quit earlier through the overwhelm of short-term pain.

To ensure mental wellness, take heed of the power of mindfulness to prevent negative moments escalating beyond control. Every time you feel overwhelmed, make a mistake, or fall victim to negative events, try to contextualize your position and realize that the chimp is behind most of the negative emotions. Apply the techniques explained throughout this book to help reign in the chimp, reassert the dominance of the rational human part of the brain, and mitigate the feelings of mental stress and anxiety from the source. Secondly, do not underestimate the importance of social interactions in maintaining a healthy mental state. A distinct lack of social interactions will release chemicals intended to force you back into the safety of the herd. This cannot be wished away no matter how mindful one is of it. It can only be quenched by fulfilling these chemical needs for social interaction. The mind and body are synergistic; when one suffers so too will the other.

4.5 Practice Good Posture

The modern demands of life are not predisposed to promote good posture. Sitting in an office chair or behind the wheel of a vehicle for hours on end are now common working environments, but they often wreak havoc on the body's natural musculoskeletal equilibrium. In fact, if you find yourself sitting in the same position for more than just a few hours at a time, detrimental effects on your posture are almost a certainty.

A national survey by Orlando Health finds that too few Americans are concerned with the health effects of bad posture. This is deeply concerning considering how extensive and debilitating the effects of poor posture often are. Back, neck, and shoulder pain are amongst the most common complaints, with poor posture usually a root cause. Sitting at a desk often results in shoulders hunching forward and the neck tilted down. Sitting like this for extended periods will result in this position becoming the new norm as the shoulder and chest muscles tighten and the muscles of the back, shoulders, and neck lengthen and weaken. Sitting also tightens the hip flexors in the front of the hips and lengthens (weakens) the glutes and hamstrings, creating the infamous "Donald Duck" posture where the butt sticks out. This may not be immediately noticeable to you, but anyone trained in muscular systems can spot this imbalance a mile away.

If left untreated, these tight muscles pull on the underlying skeletal system. The spine is a critically important and delicate system that needs to be kept in its optimal range of motion for long term health. The spine itself is rarely the source of the problem, rather it is the surrounding muscles that contort the spine into unnatural positions as they become tight, weak, and unbalanced. Over time this contortion will wear the cartilage and bone in the spine as it moves in impinged ranges of motion, often resulting in permanent damage. Curvature of the spine is a common sight these days, especially in the elderly. Chances are these people were subject to poor posture at some point in their lives and are now victim to its long-term effects.

I too, fell victim to the effects of poor posture during my years at university. Eight hours a day sitting in lecture halls or behind a desk, combined with many hours of cycling (in a hunched forward position) curved my lower and upper spine significantly as my hip flexors tightened and glutes weakened, resulting in anterior pelvic tilt (hips tilting forward). I constantly suffered from lower backache, made worse by my attempts to lift heavyweights in the gym. My tightened muscles, caused by sustained exposure to positions of poor posture, pulled my spine out of its natural alignment to the point where even the simple act of walking became uncomfortable.

Back and neck pain are strong indicators that poor posture may be putting unnatural pressure on your musculoskeletal system. The only way to combat these issues is the same way as they were accumulated; spending time rebalancing muscular imbalances and resetting the nervous system. If your shoulders hunch forward, the chest and shoulders need to be stretched whilst the weakened muscles of the back are simultaneously strengthened to support this new range of motion. Similarly, an anterior pelvic tilt, a common problem caused by sitting for extended periods of time, can be combated by stretching the hip flexors and quads in the front of your pelvis whilst strengthening the weakened glutes and hamstrings in the rear. What is most important, however, is recognizing exactly what is causing your poor posture in the first place, such as sitting for extended periods, and making sure this root cause is addressed. When sitting at a desk, for example, make an effort to periodically check if your shoulders are slumped forward and pull them back. Stand up every hour or so and take a quick walk to ensure the hip flexors and quads do not tighten. The nervous system needs to relearn good posture and the only way to do this is to manually enforce it over time.

Massage therapy can be incredibly beneficial for addressing muscle imbalances. Shortened muscles tend to be tight and cramped. When shortened for extended periods of time, they will ultimately "knot", leading to painful trigger points. Only physical manipulation through massage therapy can effectively untangle these knots and allow the muscles to maintain the correct positioning needed to hold a healthy posture.

Ultimately, the permanent elimination of poor posture requires avoiding these unhealthy positions in the first place. Pragmatically, this isn't completely avoidable when work environments require us to sit for most of the day. So, we have to make the concerted effort to counter the ill effects through active movements.

Taking a walking break every hour, or simply standing and moving the legs to ensure blood can circulate around the body, goes a long way. Regularly stretch those muscles, which are at risk of tightening, even if just for a couple of minutes every hour or so. After work hours in the gym or on the yoga mat at home should be dedicated to ensuring you reverse the tightening effects of sitting throughout the day.

I cannot stress how important it is to maintain good posture. Muscle imbalances caused by poor posture will magnify into old age. A slightly hunched neck and shoulders will become debilitating in old age, resulting in extreme immobility as seen in many elderly people. Muscle imbalances in the legs will eventually weaken the knees and possibly see you spend the remainder of your life in a wheelchair. Your future quality of life truly depends on how well you can maintain good posture whilst you're still able to.

5. Finance

5.1 Save Hard and Save Early

It is universally accepted that saving money for later on in life is sensible, whether it be for retirement or sending children to college. Yet most still fail to save anywhere near enough. In the U.S. just 16 percent save more than 15 percent of their income - an amount experts generally recommend for healthy retirement savings. Payday arrives and the temptation to spend is irresistible. This frivolous spending is often justified by arguing what the point of life is when one cannot indulge themself having dedicated most of their waking hours working a job that isn't of any real interest. Surely, it's better to spend money and enjoy it while you are still young and more able to appreciate it?

Although harmful to your financial future, these thoughts are not surprising when thinking about human behavior on a biological level. Humans are naturally wired to do things wrong with money. The vast majority of human history has been spent in hunter-gatherer societies, where resources were plentiful and only what could be carried was worth saving. We are therefore not really hardwired to collect more than we need for the next few days. In the summer bears eat all the salmon they can forage. They do not care about getting fat or the cardiovascular effects of carrying all that weight. All they care about is obtaining enough calories to survive the next winter. Saving for the future is a relatively new concept in our evolution so the ability to purposely delay gratification and save for the long, distant future is just not something that comes naturally to us. Instead, we have to be very aware of the importance of saving and go out of our way to put in place steps that ensure we consistently save.

Whilst most acknowledge that saving is important, few truly understand the importance and immense power of saving hard and, in particular, saving early. If they did, they almost certainly wouldn't lease a brand-new German car after just a couple of months of working, as seems to be the trend in an era of low-interest car leases.

Apart from the obvious financial advantages, savings afford you a higher degree of freedom over those who have none. Your savings, believe it or not, affect the way you stand, the way you walk, and ultimately your physical well-being and self-confidence. A person without savings is always running. They must take the first job offered, no matter how much they might not want to. They have no options; without cash, they cannot afford the basic essentials. They always feel on edge as any unforeseen event can throw them into financial despair. Savings are a powerful tool to buy a greater degree of freedom. If your boss frustrates you or applies unfair pressure at work, you have the option of walking away without worrying about the next six months' bills. Even if you don't, the knowledge that you would at least be able to financially is very reassuring and mitigates a lot of potential anxiety. If your car starts giving you problems, you have the option to fix or replace it. The freedom that options provide is invaluable and relinquishes so much mental anxiety that many other equally hard-working people must suffer through every day. When living paycheck-to-paycheck, you're really just an indentured worker, because while you can technically quit your job, there is immense pressure not to. That's financial duress.

Saving young also imprints good financial discipline that you will carry with you through the rest of life. Offspring also tend to pick up financial habits from their parents, meaning you are also investing in your child's future by instilling good financial practice. Those who have savings in the U.S. have also been found to live longer on average. The life expectancy for a man born in 1950, for example, is 73 for the poorest 10 percent but 87 for the richest 10 percent. A similar gap was also found for women. There could be a myriad of reasons why this is the case, but wealthier people are statistically more likely to be happier and healthier.

The number of people without sufficient retirement funds is frightening. The average pension pot for those aged between 55-64 in the US is just $107,000. Whilst this might sound like a lot, at a typical 4 percent withdrawal rate this would result in just $357 a month to live on, for the rest of your life. A person in this category would be wholly dependent on the state social security payment of $1,503 a month, for a total income of just $1,860 a month, or $22,320 annually. Not exactly the retirement funds many would come to expect after a life of hard work. Even more worryingly, new data from Northwestern Mutual's 2019 Planning and Progress Study found that 15 percent of Americans have no retirement savings at all.

Experts recommend amassing between $500,000 and $1 million US dollars by the time of retirement for a comfortable pension income. Assuming a widely accepted withdrawal rate of 4 percent, this will leave an annual income of $20,000 for a $500,000 pot and $40,000 for a $1 million pot, plus any social security you may be entitled to. For many, this would be enough to maintain the lifestyle that they have become accustomed to, especially once mortgages and bills are paid off.

Saving such great sums for retirement may sound unrealistic, especially for lower earners. Yet there is one aspect of life that can help anyone get there; time. If you start saving at 25, you have to save roughly $500 per month to hit $1 million by retirement at age 65 (assuming a conservative 6 percent annual rate of return on pension funds). The more time this money can sit and accumulate interest, the less is needed to be contributed. Starting just 10 years later at age 35, however, would almost double the monthly contribution needed to $910. At 45, this would become an eye-watering $1850 a month.

Ironically, the most important time to start investing in your pension is in your twenties. Even younger, if possible. Such is the power of time and compound interest that it becomes exponentially more difficult to catch up with each passing decade. Saving early is the most important factor here. For many, the financial impacts of decisions are not thought through. For example, spending $500 per month on a new car lease at age 20 for two years may not seem like much. In total, this will cost $12,000 over two years. Were you to invest this same monthly contribution in a simple and safe index fund (as we will see later), this initial $12,000 would magnify into $177,361 by the time you retire at age 65. At a 4 percent average withdrawal, this would yield nearly $600 a month in interest, a payment that would be made to you for the rest of your life. With the average life expectancy of 79, this initial $500 a month car lease would wipe out nearly $110,000 in income alone. By the time you're 65, that car you bought at 20 would barely be a memory. Yet that extra monthly income would be valued for the rest of your life.

Many would argue that a car is a necessity, which may be true. But leasing a perfectly capable Toyota Camry instead of a BMW, a price difference of say 250 per month, would lead to an extra $88,680, or retirement income of $296 a month, for the rest of your life. It can be hard to think like this for many; remember humans are not hard-wired to think long term. But I guarantee when you retire and must rely on the state for survival, it will be a mistake that will haunt you all the way to your grave.

Another common mistake is dedicating the first ten working years to "living life and having fun while you're young". Whilst this is certainly important, after all, youth is one of the most valuable assets that can never be bought back, avoiding savings during these early years is a life-changing mistake. Let's look at an example:

Michael saved $1,000 per month from the time he turned 25 until he turned 35. Then he stopped saving but left his money in his investment account where it continued to accrue at a seven percent growth rate until he retired at age 65. Jennifer held off and didn't start saving until age 35. She put away $1,000 per month from her 35th birthday until she turned 45. Like Michael, she left the balance in her investment account, where it continued to accrue at a rate of seven percent until age 65. Sam didn't get around to investing until age 45. Still, he invested $1,000 per month for 10 years, halting his savings at age 55. Then he also left his money to accrue at a seven percent rate until his 65th birthday. Michael, Jennifer, and Sam each saved the same amount — $120,000 — over a 10-year period. Sadly for Jennifer, and even more so for Sam, their ending balances were dramatically different. At retirement, Michael amassed $1,444,969. Jennifer attained $734,549 and Sam ended up with just $373,407. All made the same time and monetary commitments, but the outcomes are life changing. Just by using time to his advantage, Michael became a millionaire at retirement. Sam, on the other hand, will have to rely on the state for the rest of his life. Whilst it is almost certainly more difficult to save $1000 during your 20s than it is in your 30s and 40s (which are prime earning years), the results speak for themselves and sacrifices have to be made.

Enjoyment and savings are not mutually exclusive. You do not have to forgo all sense of fun and enjoyment in order to stow money away into savings. But a compromise must be made and made as soon as possible. Leasing that slightly cheaper car or mortgaging that slightly smaller first house could be the difference between financial freedom or financial hell come retirement. Experts recommend saving between 10 percent and 15 percent of monthly paychecks into a retirement fund. This becomes increasingly more difficult the less you earn as the cost of living tends to be fixed. But whatever your position, you need to find some way of saving even $100 a month. Even this small monthly sum from 25 to 65 will grow to almost $200,000. For those who are older and are yet to start saving, you still need to maximize time as best you can by contributing as much as possible. Your future self depends on it.

5.2 Where to Save

Hopefully, the importance of saving hard and saving early is now abundantly clear. The next problem is where to direct these monthly savings? Investing is often a financial minefield of overly technical jargon and curious advice from "experts" with questionable motives. With so many investment vehicles, from savings accounts, managed funds, ETFs, equities, bonds and everything in between, optimizing your return, whilst avoiding the pitfalls of greedy fund managers and swings in the economy, can be boiled down to simple gambling for the majority of us who are not financial experts. Many, having been burned by poor stock choices their broker promised was a "sure thing", or still suffering from the impacts of the last global recession, stick cash under their mattress, or buy physical commodities such as gold and silver where they can physically see their wealth. Unfortunately, these techniques can be just as dangerous as the risks of the stock market in forgone wealth. Whether we like it or not, the stock market is the most efficient platform to build wealth for the majority. Fortunately, investing doesn't have to be complicated, or risky. Just a few extremely simple practices will turn your hard-earned cash into as close to a risk-free return as is possible.

There are three fundamental principles that must be understood prior to investing. The first is that return on investment and risk are most often inversely correlated. High reward vehicles, such as Real Estate Investment Funds (REITs), can yield a tasty 10-15 percent, but they are considered fairly high risk and volatile. On the other hand, savings accounts are as close to risk-free as is possible, with most accounts insured by the state. For example, the U.S. FDIC insures individual savings accounts up to $250,000. Unfortunately, this safety is offset by a poor interest rate of around 0.09 percent.

The second principle is that your money should always be invested in a channel that offers the benefit of compound interest. Einstein once quipped that "compound interest is the eighth wonder of the world". It is the fundamental principle used by all wealthy people to make their money work for them. Compound interest is the addition of interest to the principal sum of a loan or deposit, or in other words, interest on interest. It is the result of reinvesting interest, rather than paying it out, so that interest in the next period is then earned on the principal sum plus previously accumulated interest. Sounds complicated but any investment which earns you interest, which you can then reinvest to earn further interest, is compounding. This is why holding commodities such as gold, art, and classic cars will rarely meet the returns that the stock market will long-term; commodities are essentially another bet that their value will rise. There is no income aspect to them either, so when their value drops, you lose. Compound interest, on the other hand, still earns an income even when the stock market is decreasing (you still always earn interest unless your initial sum goes to zero), just at a lesser rate, so even when the stock market decreases, you are still building wealth.

Thirdly, it is imperative that you invest for the long term and do not get greedy. There is almost no reliable get rich quick scheme that is inherently safe. Yes, some get lucky, but for reliable results, compounding offers the only guaranteed building of wealth. But compounding depends on time; a pension should be accumulated over decades. Many start investing with good intentions but get scared when the market flounders and sell. The investment vehicles I will show you, however, rely on you keeping your money in the stock market when times are good and when times are bad. It relies on the historical notion that the stock market always rises over long time spans (decades). So, you need to prepare yourself for the fact that your investments will ebb and flow with the market in general. Some years you will lose and some you will win. But you will always win in the long term because of the tried and tested value of compound interest.

There are three key investment vehicles everyone should utilize, no matter the country. Only after maximizing these three investments can one justifiably spend on luxuries and frivolous purchases.

Firstly, you should place all available disposable income into acquiring six months of living expenses to create an emergency fund. This is preached by many but practiced by few. And in times of a viral pandemic, where jobs are lost overnight, reserving funds for unexpected moments such as these have never been more relevant. Living expenses differ by circumstance; a family of four will have much greater living expenses than a single person. Living expenses include your monthly housing costs, food, health care, utilities, transport, and debt. Some claim it should be six months' salary but the very minimum should be six months of expenses, i.e. you should be able to live for 6 months if the worst were to happen and you had zero income. Six months is enough time for most to get back on their feet. For me personally, this amounts to $16,000. This contingency fund allows for any unforeseen and sudden changes to your personal living situation, such as a medical emergency or loss of a job.

This money should be highly liquid (accessible as cash at any moment), ideally in a savings account. Interest rates on these are typically low, often lower than inflation, but it is instant access that is the priority; any interest is just a bonus. A savings account in this economic climate might earn a measly 1 percent interest annually and not even keep up with inflation, which tends to run between 2-3 percent a year. You may even have to pay taxes on your meager 1 percent earnings. However, anything is better than the 0 percent it earns as cash or going into credit card debt, which can charge 10-30 percent interest. Remember, the sole point of this cash is to have instant access to six months of living expenses in case of an emergency, providing not only financial support but mental confidence in your financial position. A savings account, despite measly returns, also abides by our first investment principle; always invest your money where it can benefit from compounding interest. Once this emergency fund has reached the six-month mark as determined by your personal situation, you can stop contributing to it and simply leave it there to collect interest and be available at any moment.

The second avenue to spend your disposable income, after building your emergency fund, is contributing to any workplace pension plans that may be offered by your employer. This differs by country and level of job but the principles are the same. In the UK it is now mandatory for all employers to offer a pension plan to employees. The legal minimum that must be paid into a pension is 8 percent a year of qualifying earnings, of which at least 3 percent must be paid by the employer. The usual split is 5 percent from employees and 3 percent from employers. This means by investing 5 percent of your salary, your company will top up your pension contribution by an additional 3 percent. This extra 3 percent is effectively free money and should be maximized. As an added bonus, this contributed money usually comes out of your pre-tax income (in the UK), effectively boosting your contribution even further. To not capitalize on this is absolutely wasteful.

In the US, a similar system is used in the form of a 401k, except the employer is not mandated to contribute any percentage. The average US 401k contribution is around 8 percent, matching the UK contribution (although those lucky Brits only have to contribute 5 percent of their own income to receive this 8 percent). Many US employers, however, will match your contribution up to a certain percentage. Again, this is free pre-tax money and must be taken, so check with your employer as to how much they are willing to match and ensure you maximize it fully. It is worth noting that if you are self-employed, there are options available to you as well, such as a solo 401k or a SIPP in the UK. Although there is no employer to match contributions, there are at least tax advantages to them. Whatever your employer offers, match sure you contribute enough to receive the maximum employer contribution.

Once you have set up your emergency fund and maximized your workplace pension contributions, the third investment stream should be a personal investment vehicle capitalizing on any tax-advantaged accounts your country may offer. In the UK, everyone can invest up to £20,000 a year in an Individual Savings Account (ISA). Any interest accrued on these investments is completely tax-free for life, making them an incredibly efficient way to invest. This limit renews every year, meaning you can contribute up to £20,000 each year. This is beyond the reach of many people, but you should try to maximize as much as you can on this tax-free investment vehicle.

Again, the U.S. has a similar vehicle called an Individual Retirement Account (IRA). There are two main types: traditional IRAs and Roth IRAs which are similar but taxed differently. Traditional IRAs allow you to deduct the amount contributed from your pre-tax income. The advantage here is that you defer your tax payments until later in life when you retire, a point in life where most people earn less (and therefore pay less tax). The US is less generous in these vehicles than the UK with the annual limit set at $6,000 ($7,000 for over 50s). This would be the personal investment vehicle of choice for most Americans. Canadians have a similar vehicle called a Registered Retirement Savings Plan (RRSP) which allows participants to contribute up to 18 percent of earned income up to a maximum of $26,500. These types of accounts, with their favorable tax advantages, should be maximized alongside workplace pensions to build up sufficient retirement funds for a comfortable life post-retirement.

Whereas pension plans are automatically managed by your company's pension provider, individual tax-advantaged investments need to be managed by you. This leaves many (understandably) overwhelmed as to where to invest their money. Most are not experts in the stock market and therefore rightly stay away from it. There is one investment vehicle, however, that is extremely safe and offers one of the best compromises of risk vs. reward on the market; Index funds.

Index funds have only really become popular in the last few decades as amateur investors, such as myself, have come to the realization that they offer the most reliably safe return on investment in the stock market. They are now so popular that as of 2016, more than $1 out of every $5 invested in the equity markets in the U.S. was believed to be invested through the conduit of an index fund. An index is a measurement of a section of the stock market. For example, in the U.S. the most popular indexes are the S&P 500, which contains the 500 largest companies in the U.S. economy weighted by market capitalization, and the Dow Jones Industrial Average which is a collection of 30 companies that are selected to represent their respective industries. An index fund therefore sets to mimic the entire index. For example, buying an index fund of the S&P 500 will buy a little piece of (almost) every single company in that index. Your results will therefore follow the index exactly, meaning you perform no worse or no better than it does. Since the S&P 500's inception in 1957, the index has averaged an annual return of 8 percent. That is a pretty good return for minimal risk. There is absolutely no reason to believe that this return won't continue for the next 60 years.

The benefits of index funds are numerous. Firstly, they are about as safe a position as you can hold in the stock market, as long as your investment window is long term (decades) which it should be (remember investment principle number 3). Whereas individual stocks are highly volatile and susceptible to complete loss, index funds spread your bets across hundreds of companies. Index funds track the index they follow, meaning the only way to lose your money is if the stock market completely collapses. The only realistic way for this to happen is through the total collapse of the financial system, such as the total annihilation of the U.S. through war or a natural pandemic. In this situation, you would have substantially greater problems than your retirement savings.

Index funds are extremely passive and take a set and forget type approach. You simply set up a monthly contribution to your find of choice, forget about it, and let time and compound interest do the hard work for you. Remember we are investing for the long term, ideally in the decades. The stock market, and hence your index fund, will ebb and flow with the financial tides but the long-term results will mirror the average rise of its respective index for a historical average of between 7 and 9 percent. Some years you may lose 20 percent, others you may gain 20. Even if your index fund is down 50 percent, the power of compounding will still make you money. You don't need to allocate any time or effort in maintaining your investments, you simply need to open an account, pick your index fund, and set up a monthly transfer.

The battle is now heating up between passive funds, such as index funds, and actively managed funds, such as the typical mutual funds where you hand over your money to investment experts who handpick their own set of stocks using years of "insider knowledge" and "expertise"). Whilst managed funds can be more profitable short term if you are lucky, long term trends actually show index funds to be more profitable. 2019 marked the 9th consecutive year that the majority (64.49 percent) of actively managed funds lagged the S&P 500. After 10 years, 85 percent of actively managed funds underperformed the S&P 500, and after 15 years, nearly 92 percent trailed the index. This gap increases the longer the time span. In our holding period of 40 years or more, the chances of an active fund outperforming a passive index fund tend close to zero. What's more, fund managers require fees of up to 1 percent. Passive index funds, on the other hand, require little maintenance and fees can be as low as 0.1 percent. This small difference can result in tens of thousands once compounded over 40 years.

The most popular index fund in the U.S. is the Vanguard 500 Index (VFINX) which has an expense ratio of just 0.14 percent and the minimum initial investment is $3,000. The Schwab S&P 500 Index (SWPPX) is another popular choice and performs much the same. These can be purchased through investment platforms open to anyone, such as Fidelity, Charles Schwab, and E*Trade. Look for whichever platform has the lowest fees. Each country will have its own investment platform and index fund, so research the best platforms for your specific geography. Remember to open these index funds in whatever tax-efficient account your country offers. For the U.S. these would be IRAs, for Canada they would be RRSPs and the UK ISAs. Aim to maximize these annual contribution limits as much as possible.

These basic principles, even if you can only contribute just $50 or $100 a month, will leave you in a much healthier financial position than many others. One of the best advantages is that they are all passive; you just set up an automatic monthly transfer and forget about them until retirement. From here time and compound interest do all the hard work for you.

5.3 Think of Money in Terms of Labor

Since the dawn of modern civilization, man has traded his labor for currency. Whether it be the modern U.S. dollar or dolphin's teeth on the Solomon Islands, the modern economy depends on this basic exchange. Since money is most often earned by selling labor, it makes sense to think of expenses in terms of time and labor too. The physical currency itself is just the middleman and is only as intrinsically valuable as the paper it's printed on. The true value lies in how much time must be dedicated in order to acquire it.

How do you determine whether an item is worth purchasing or not? Many judge this simply by the value of their bank accounts; if they can afford it, they will buy it. This is perhaps not surprising considering humans are inherently wired to think short-term like their hunter-gatherer ancestors. Those new sneakers may spike your emotions for pleasure, but will you still value them the same in a few months' time? Often the case is no, and people either return the item or live with the guilt. The chimp also makes these decisions difficult; the emotional part of your brain may be excited by the thought of racing around in a new sports car, but when the high monthly payments start rolling in, and the initial thrill of the new car wears off, the rational human part of the brain may start to regret the decision.

So how can we make better decisions about particular purchases before it is too late? One of the best ways I have found is to look at the "time value of money". This approach looks at cost not only in terms of numerical value (which intrinsically means very little) but also in terms of how much time would have to be worked in order to earn it. For example, let's assume your salary is a little above the U.S average at $200 a day, or $25 an hour for an average eight-hour working day. That morning $3 coffee may not seem a lot, but you would have to work for more than seven minutes to earn it. Would you work seven extra minutes for a cup of coffee? Quite possibly; if that extra seven minutes of work helps give you a much-needed caffeine boost to help you be more productive during the day, then go for it. If you could make coffee in the office and go home seven minutes earlier, would you trade this? There is no correct answer and it depends solely on the individual; some would appreciate the time value of a coffee more than others.

Consider spending a night in a hotel. Upgrading to a premium room might cost you $400. Not bad for a special occasion, right? Now consider this in terms of your labor. That upgrade over a regular $200 room would mean you would have a whole day just to pay for this upgrade. Would you work an extra day for this short-lived upgrade? Again, the answer depends on the individual. Perhaps you're at a restaurant and your chimp is telling you to purchase that expensive glass of wine at $25. Would you work an hour for these few sips?

This line of thinking can also apply in the opposite extreme. I remember toying with the idea of purchasing an annual ski pass for C$1000. Being the tight sod that I am, the high value alone was enough to almost put me off. Yet when I analyzed it in terms of my labor (I was earning the equivalent of $200 a day), this worked out to be one week's labor in exchange for four months of unlimited skiing.

Additionally, it was a great time to hang out with work colleagues who later became very good friends and expanded my professional network. Although the dollar value was high, the time value was modest. The same applied for my weekly massages; at $100 for a weekly session, the dollar value per hour seemed high. Yet when considering the benefits, such as a healthy and ache-free body for as long as I kept this up, the equivalent time value of half a day per week became reasonable to me.

I have used a $25 hourly wage as a benchmark, but this value will be different for many. Yet everyone is on the same playing field in terms of time; everyone gets just 24 hours in a day. So, converting value into terms of time gives a fair comparison for all. For those high earners earning $500 a day, a high end $100 meal will take just a couple of hours to pay off. For someone earning minimum wage, this would equate to a whole day's labor.

Next time you are pondering a purchase, first understand that your inner chimp, with its natural penchant for impulse spending based on emotion, is most likely at play. Convert the price into your time value of money based on how many hours/days you would have to work in order to pay for it. Evaluate whether you would be happy to work this extra amount of time to have this item. This line of thinking helps distract the chimp's immediate urge for gratification with the urge to not have to work unpleasant hours in order to pay for it. It also allows for a different perspective of value that may help clarify your decision, and save you from making a regretful decision.

5.4 Identify the Two Types of Spending - Hedonic and Utilitarian

We have all succumbed to the impulse purchase of items we later regret. From clothes, food, and flashy new cars, what seemed like a good idea at the time often morphs into the realization that we let emotion get the better of us. It is not all our fault, however. Retailers understand these trends all too well and manipulate it to squeeze every cent out of us as best they can. Ever wonder why checkout isles are full of chocolate and candies? These highly impulsive products are specifically placed right in front of the buyer in the hopes of latching onto their highly impulsive natures.

Consumers spend $5,400 per year on average on impulse purchases of food, clothing, household items, and shoes. This equates to $15 a day on random items we had no intention of buying until they were shoved under our noses. In fact, most spontaneous purchases involve eating; 70.5 percent of respondents in a recent survey named food as their biggest impulse purchase. At the same time, 85 percent of survey respondents said their impulse purchase involved taking advantage of a deal or discount, another favorite tactic used by retailers to part us with more of our hard-earned cash.

Retailers have developed a science behind this concept, which I learned from a successful retail magnate friend of mine. Her job was to get people to purchase as much as possible and as quickly as possible every time a consumer shopped online. According to the Baymard Institute, 68 percent of online shopping carts are abandoned once consumers have had their fun indulging their impulsive shopping needs and, upon seeing the total price on checkout, abandoned the shop. Her job was to understand shoppers' motivations in order to build a relationship with consumers and convert them into valuable customers. She outlined the two types of purchases all consumers make; hedonic and utilitarian.

Utilitarian shopping is all about actual need and function. We need clothes, we need food, we need dental floss — and utilitarian motives drive these needs. Our utilitarian motives for shopping include: meeting our basic needs, finding greater convenience, seeking variety, seeking a greater quality of merchandise, and searching for better prices. For these shoppers, purchasing is a problem-solving activity that follows a series of logical steps. There is very little emotion involved in these purchases so the rational human part of the brain is more likely to be driving decisions than the emotional chimp. These sorts of shoppers are accommodated for by retailers but not manipulated; it is extremely hard to draw money from someone who is not emotionally involved in the shopping process. Cell plans, grocery shopping, electricity bills, and rent are all in this category. Our primary goal here is to find the best value for money.

On the other hand, hedonic shopping is driven by a desire for fun, entertainment, and satisfaction. It's derived from the perceived fun or playfulness of shopping experiences. Hedonic shopping stirs emotional arousal within us — both physiological and psychological. The individual is deeply involved in the satisfaction of shopping, and the higher the level of involvement, the greater the level of hedonism experienced by the shopper.

Hedonic shopping is what leads to impulse spending. For example, you have a shopping list of all groceries and household items you need to purchase for the week. As they are all essentials, this shop should be utilitarian. When shopping, however, you stumble across the candy aisle and suddenly find your trolley full of chocolate. We have all been there. These impulse items were not planned and based on rational and logical needs but on emotion and immediate impulses. The candy is therefore hedonic. Hedonic shopping is not limited to just food; automobiles, in particular, can be as much an emotional purchase as a rational one. This lead auto-dealers all over the world to market their products in a rapid-fire, almost carnival-like manner designed to appeal to emotion over reason.

Some people are inherently more susceptible to hedonic impulse purchasing than others. Academic research that explores the various triggers of impulse buying consists of two main schools of thought. First, some scholars argue that individual traits lead consumers to engage in impulse buying. For example, people who are naturally more impulsive in life are more likely to engage in impulse buying. Among the psychological factors that might evoke impulse buying, researchers have explored the traits of sensation seeking, impulsivity, and representations of self-identity. Second, both motives and resources might drive impulse buying. Researchers have identified the effects of the two types of motives (hedonic and utilitarian), as well as subjective norms, and argued that mere impulsiveness is often not strong enough to trigger impulse buying. Instead, the availability of resources coupled with a failure of self-control also is required to enact impulse buying.

A typical scenario of these two types of purchases can be seen in selecting a cell phone contract. A typical consumer might dedicate an hour or so to finding the very best deal for them, weighing up options such as the number of calls, texts, internet usage, and cost to find the optimum contract. A $15 monthly difference between two contracts is a big deal and would cause most consumers to swap contracts immediately. Yet the average consumer doesn't think twice about spending $15 on coffee every month which provides little to no long-term value. Cell phone contracts invoke little emotion and are therefore utilitarian. Coffee purchases are driven by your emotion for immediate gratification (not necessarily negative, however, they offer value in terms of pleasure) and are therefore a hedonic purchase. $15 is always $15, yet we value them differently when it comes to the two types of spending.

Both types of spending are natural, yet people understandably tend to lean too much toward the hedonic type. To help balance the two, there are some general tips which can be applied while shopping.

First, be mindful as to which type of purchase you are making. Mindfulness is the most powerful first step in gaining control over the emotional chimp. Acknowledge that emotion is currently driving decisions and that it is perfectly natural to feel this way. Once the chimp has vented, and you have successfully distracted or boxed it, use the rational aspect of your brain to ask if this item will add value to your life past the initial satisfaction? Will it provide any longer-term value? Longer-term doesn't have to mean days in the future; that coffee first thing in the morning might provide long term benefits in preparing you better for the day ahead.

Secondly, shop with a goal. Plan your purchases and stick to them. Create a strict list before shopping to only include the things you need, and plan your route throughout the stores to get these items to avoid walking past unnecessary temptations. Walking into a store with an open mind is like walking in there with an open checkbook. A plan of action takes the emotion out of the scenario and avoids drifting off towards rogue purchases.

Thirdly, create a seven-day waiting list for big purchases. After one week, if you are still thinking about the product and still feel like it would benefit you, it most likely isn't a complete impulse buy. If you are no longer interested in the product after a week, you probably avoided making an unnecessary impulse buy. The more valuable the purchase, the more time may be needed to sit on it and let the emotion ruminate.

Conclusion

If you're still with me at this point, congratulations. There is a lot of information to process and it cannot be digested in just one sitting. This information represents an entire lifetimes' worth of knowledge and experience that will require a similar amount of time for you to master. It is up to you to use the tools provided to act upon what is preached.

The sheer amount of information may seem overwhelming. But fear not, for we already know how to deal with overwhelm. Create a plan that will enable you to tackle each chapter in bite-sized segments which you can begin to tackle immediately. Focus on one of two topics at a time - reread these chapters whilst thinking of ways in which you can practice them regularly.

Download my habit building table document (or create your own) and create those productive habits you've always wanted to. Start slowly and build upon them incrementally; remember, progress takes time. Success results from the systematic application of fundamental concepts and principles that facilitate consistent progress. The emphasis should always be on incremental improvements as opposed to sheer results. Success requires a strong foundation first, not the other way around.

As you improve in each of these areas, you will begin to fix your metaphoric cracks and strengthen your foundation. And the stronger your foundation, the better your ability to overcome and adapt to any challenge. This foundation will not only help you achieve your specific goals but will aid your competence in all walks of life. The momentum of self-improvement will see your confidence soar, with each small success accumulating into a new sense of confidence that will help you forever. Like a snowball at the top of a mountain, all you need is that little starting push. Once rolling, however, the size of the snowball increases at an exponential rate. So take yourself to the top of the mountain and practice the advice presented in this book to give yourself that first little push.

Thank you for taking the time to read my book. I hope it helps you on your journey through life as much as it has helped me.

If you would like to remain informed of any upcoming book releases, please join the community and sunscribe to the link below.

Thanks again!

https://jason-strong.ck.page

9 781999 922734